Storms Are Faith's Workout

Storm's Are Faith's Workout

Preparing Christians for Spiritual Ambush

R. C. JETTE

RESOURCE *Publications* • Eugene, Oregon

STORMS ARE FAITH'S WORKOUT
Preparing Christians for Spiritual Ambush

Resource Publications
An Imprint of Wipf and Stock Publishers
199 W. 8th Ave., Suite 3
Eugene, OR 97401

www.wipfandstock.com

PAPERBACK ISBN: 978-1-5326-6459-5
HARDCOVER ISBN: 978-1-5326-6460-1
EBOOK ISBN: 978-1-5326-6461-8

Manufactured in the U.S.A.   SEPTEMBER 27, 2018

This book is dedicated to my Lord Jesus Christ! To God be the glory, for without him I would be overcome in the storms of life.

The Lord also will be a refuge for the oppressed, a refuge in times of trouble. And they that know thy name will put their trust in thee; for thou, Lord, hast not forsaken them that seek thee (Psalms 9:9–10).

Contents

Introduction

To write a first book at seventy-one years of age is a storm in itself, for I am all at sea. But when the Lord prompts you to do something, obedience should be your next move. He has impressed upon my heart that He is concerned about the spiritual storms assailing his children. It seems that Christians are being ambushed daily by the enemy of their souls and are trodden down with depression and discouragement. Many are losing heart and have stopped fighting. In fact, some have become tired of running the race.

In almost forty years of ministering and counseling, never has this reality become more obvious than it is today. I am no novice to the troubles afflicting the Body of Christ. And I am no stranger to storms, for I have endured many ruthless ambushes by the enemy.

To support my claim to those of you reading this book, I will give a few examples. When I was a very young Christian, my twenty-six-year-old brother committed suicide. Later on, my mother and fifty-one-year-old brother passed away within three months of each other. My seven-year-old granddaughter passed away. My youngest daughter was brutally attacked, and now suffers the results of strangulation. A lack of employment caused mounting debt. I was hospitalized for diverticulosis, ulcerated colitis, kidney stone, and 2.4 potassium level. I hurt my neck and was bedridden for about two years. That should be enough to suffice any doubting Thomas.

I believe that I know and understand storms, and that is the basis for the Lord prompting me to write this book. Through my storms, He has given me spiritual insight into how to overcome all storms that try to destroy the faith of his children.

This perception has been gained through the storms that I have encountered in my spiritual journey to Heaven. It is not bought for a song; for it comes through unremitting persistence. If it had come easily, I would not know its value. I have always held to the truth that the things that are worked for are the things that are cherished the most. I am not talking about working for my salvation. What I am implying is the knowledge and wisdom that is gained through reading and studying my Bible, and then living that knowledge and wisdom during the storms. It is a daily application of what has been learned.

Only those reading this book who are eager to have a scriptural basis to build upon will truly understand how to endure and overcome the enemy's storms. However, I pray that those who were not enthusiastic upon endeavoring to read will come away with transformed insight and wisdom from the truth of God's word that will enable them to become over comers.

As I look around, I am convinced that this is the hour for such a book. In its pages are revealed strategies of the devil and how to stand during the most savage storms. It is a modest endeavor, but its fruit will be seen in the life of the person who reads and adheres to its advice and wisdom.

I have one goal for writing such a book, and it is for you the reader. You have picked up this book, because you are in storms. You feel as though there is no way out, and you do not know how long you can endure. Be patient and read the wisdom enclosed. There are no shortcuts to overcoming, just as there are no shortcuts to Heaven. It will take an effort on your part to read through to the end of the book, but you should come away much wiser and more prepared for the enemy's storms.

Jesus loves you. He has heard your cries for help. You are never alone; for He has been with you through it all. He has felt your pain. He has felt your loneliness. He has tried to comfort you. But you are so confused, that you do not understand his word. This book is his help for you to finally comprehend and stand firm during the storms.

Chapter 1

Storms Are the Test of Faith

> That the trial of your faith, being much more precious than of gold that perisheth, though it be tried with fire, might be found unto praise and honour and glory at the appearing of Jesus Christ (I Peter 1:7).

WHY IS IT SO important that a book should be written about storms? The answer is quite simple. Many Christians are ill prepared for the storms that come upon them almost daily. It is like the hurricanes that hit Puerto Rico last year. They were unprepared for such storms, and they are still trying to recover from Maria's devastation. Likewise, multitudes in the Body of Christ have been ambushed with furious storms, and like the Puerto Ricans have yet to recover. The sad truth is that many Christians are not even striving to come back; they have ceased fighting and they have quit running. This book is meant to help those who have given up to pick themselves back up and continue what they started for the Lord.

> And the same day, when the even was come, he saith unto them, Let us pass over unto the other side. And when they had sent away the multitude, they took him even as he was in the ship. And there were also with him other little ships. And there arose a great storm of wind, that the waves beat into the ship, so that it was now full. And he was in the hinder part of the ship, asleep on a

pillow: and they awake him, and say unto him, Master,
carest thou not that we perish? And he arose, and rebuked the wind, and said unto the sea, Peace, be still.
And the wind ceased, and there was a great calm. And he
said unto them, Why are ye so fearful? how is it that ye
have no faith (Mark 4:35–40)?

The above verses in the gospel of Mark will be my nucleus
for this book. In it are discovered vital points that will help us
understand storms. There are so many factors involved in order
to comprehend the difference between being prepared and being
unprepared for any storm that hits. That is why I will carefully construct the necessary information chapter by chapter. Each chapter
will build upon the previous one to enlighten our understanding.
Please bear with me, as it is imperative that I build slowly upon
each previous chapter.

At present, I want us to turn our attention to verse 35. In this
verse, Jesus gives a word or a promise to, *"Let us pass over unto the
other side."* It is imperative, it is mandatory that we understand that
any time that a word from the Lord is given, storms will follow.
This truth is the basis for this book, and one that many Christians
have not heard or do not understand. Storms are not probable in a
Christian's life, they are sure and certain. We can be as assured of
storms as we are of the sun rising and setting each day. Knowing
this truth is the beginning of being prepared.

The majority of the time when we believe God for the word
or promise, it seems like we are engulfed in a tornado, hurricane,
tsunami, and earthquake simultaneously. In other words, we feel
as though all hell has broken out against us. If truth be told, hell
has unleashed its fury against us, but that truth will be addressed
in chapter five.

When the storm is raging, we can find ourselves reacting
like the disciples in verses 37–38. The storm is violent, and fear
has engulfed us with a strangle hold. We feel as though we will
not overcome this. We are full of uncertainties, and we begin to
question whether or not we really heard from God. Did God really
say that? Did God really promise that? Did God really say to go

there? Does God really want me to do that? Did God really say to give that? None of it makes any sense. How could God have said that? It goes against all reason and logic. He couldn't have meant to literally walk on water. He couldn't have meant to cross a raging sea. How can this be done? With all these questions racing through our mind, we can feel the fear and doubt trying to consume us. However, this is not the time for questions of doubt; it is the time to stand by faith.

When we give into the fear, questions, and doubt, we are right where the devil wants us to be. We are full of negative and faithless thoughts. Remember in Genesis 3:1 when the devil asked Eve, *"Yea, hath God said?"* That's all it took, and we are all experiencing the results of the fall of man. Storms are all the evidence that we need that the devil got the victory that day. Nonetheless, this book should reveal that he doesn't have to be triumphant over us. We choose to be the victors or the victim during any storm the devil wields our way. Stay with me to the end of this book, before you cast judgment.

Let's start our pathway to overcoming our storms by viewing a few examples of storms in others from the scriptures. Each reveals that storms followed a word or a promise from the Lord.

> And Joseph dreamed a dream, and he told it his brethren: and they hated him yet the more. And he said unto them, Hear, I pray you, this dream which I have dreamed: For, behold, we were binding sheaves in the field, and lo, my sheaf arose, and also stood upright; and, behold, your sheaves stood round about, and made obeisance to my sheaf. And his brothers said to him, Shalt thou indeed reign over us? or shalt thou indeed have dominion over us? And they hated him yet the more for his dreams, and for his words. And he dreamed yet another dream, and told it his brethren, and said, Behold, I have dreamed a dream more; and, behold, the sun and the moon and the eleven stars made obeisance to me. And he told it to his father, and to his brethren: and his father rebuked him, and said unto him, What is this dream that thou hast dreamed? Shall I and thy mother and thy brethren

indeed come to bow down ourselves to thee to the earth? And his brethren envied him; but his father observed the saying (Genesis 37:1-8).

The other references concerning Joseph and his storms are found in Genesis 37:12-36 and chapters 39-50.

At this time, let's observe Joseph. He has two dreams. The fact that he has two dreams is a confirmation or witness that God would most certainly make the events happen. It is important to note that Joseph is only seventeen years of age at this point in time. He has his dreams and conveys their contents to his brothers and to his father. Understand here, Joseph has received a word or a promise from the Lord and then comes the storm or the test of faith. He finds himself almost immediately ambushed and in an onslaught of storms. His jealous brothers decide to kill him. They cast him into a pit, and Judah convinces them to sell him into slavery instead of slaying him (Genesis 37:12-28).

At a slave market in Egypt, an Egyptian named Potiphar buys him. Joseph finds favor with Potiphar who gives him charge over his whole household. Howbeit, he is ambushed by Potiphar's wife who casts her eyes upon him and tries to tempt him to lie with her. He exclaims, *"How then can I do this great wickedness, and sin against God?"* She then grabs his garment and accuses him of trying to come in unto her. Upon hearing the accusation, Potiphar has Joseph cast into prison (Genesis 39:1-20).

I want to stop and point out Joseph's life up to this time. He has done no wrong. In all this, Joseph has kept his faith and did not sin against God. He could have been overwhelmed with questions, confusion, and doubt. Although Joseph's faith was given an incredible workout, he kept his integrity, his love, and his trust in God through it all.

In prison, the Lord is with him, and Joseph finds favor with the keeper of the prison, who committed to his hand all the prisoners that were in the prison. Even in prison, Joseph still adheres to his faith in God (Genesis 39:21-23). However, just because the Lord is always with us does not mean that we will not undergo great storms or great tests of our faith. Whether Joseph was favored or not, he was still in prison. Furthermore, we saw that the Lord was with the disciples in the ship, but their unbelief caused them to fear instead of trust. Our reaction during the storms will decide our outcome.

Let's turn our attention to Joseph's outcome during his prison storm. The chief of the butlers and the chief of the bakers have troubling dreams. Joseph correctly interprets both dreams, and he asks the chief of the butlers to remember him. Two years later, when Pharaoh has his dreams, the butler remembers Joseph. Joseph interprets Pharaoh's dreams and gives him the wise counsel needed to get through the years of famine. Pharaoh is so impressed that he makes Joseph second in command over all Egypt (Genesis Chapters 40–41).

Joseph is thirty years of age when the seven years of plenty begin and thirty-seven when the seven years of famine begin. Yes, he is in a high position, but what storms he had to undergo before his promotion. He endured incredible storms year after year for no guilt. But let us not forget that the oppressive storm of not seeing his beloved father for twenty plus years had to be a remarkable storm to bear.

Allow me license in the telling of these storms about Joseph. In order for us to understand storms in our life, we have to see them in others. As I stated in the beginning, I must build layer upon layer in each chapter. If I am going to unfold how to overcome storms, I must have liberty to do it fully. At my age, I know the importance of not side stepping any vital point.

Okay, Jacob sends Joseph's brethren to buy corn in Egypt; the famine was world-wide. It is more than twenty years before Joseph's dreams are fulfilled. His brothers come before him and bow down (Genesis 42:6). Let's not forget that Joseph endured severe storms from the time that he received the word from the Lord in his dreams until their fulfillment. Yet, he never lost his rectitude, his uprightness, his honesty, his virtue, etc. with God.

Let's stop and ponder some points of this story. We all know the outcome, but Joseph did not. He has his dreams, which set him up to be hated by his jealous brothers. He is sold into slavery, which set him up to be purchased by Potiphar. If he had not been bought by Potiphar, he would not have gone to prison. If he had not been in prison, he would not have interpreted the dreams. Then he would not have been called to interpret Pharaoh's dreams, and would not have been placed second in command over all of Egypt. Sometimes, we find ourselves in a situation that has shaken our foundation. But if we learn to trust God as Joseph did; for only God knows why we are in the present predicament. His objective for all that He allows in our life is to strengthen our faith. If our faith does not get a workout, it will never be strong. As our faith in God grows stronger, we will weather any storm. Whatever the reason for the dilemma, we must be unmovable in our faith in God to get us through. This book is meant to show us how to do it.

Now, we will turn our attention to a group with a word or a promise from the Lord to go in and possess the promise land. In Exodus chapter 13, the Israelites are delivered from Egyptian bondage (a type of our being delivered from the world and the bondage of sin and death). Although delivered, the enemy immediately pursues them to bring them back into bondage. Please understand that the storms usually begin the moment that we are delivered from bondage. God promised them deliverance, and He did it. They no sooner leave Egypt, and the enemy is hot on their tail. Here comes the storm or the test of faith.

> And when Pharaoh drew nigh, the children of Israel lifted up their eyes, and, behold, the Egyptians marched after them; and they were sore afraid: and the children of Israel cried out unto the Lord. And they said unto Moses, Because there were no graves in Egypt, hast thou taken us away to die in the wilderness? wherefore hast thou dealt thus with us, to carry us forth out of Egypt? Is not this the word that we did tell thee in Egypt, saying, Let us alone, that we may serve the Egyptians? For it had been better for us to serve the Egyptians, than that we should die in the wilderness (Exodus 14:10–12).

In these verses, the Israelites are at the Red Sea with the Egyptian storm pursuing with the intention to overcome them. It is obvious that they are not like Joseph, as they have no faith in the God who brought them out of Egypt with a mighty hand. How soon they forgot their moaning and groaning to be delivered from the Egyptians. Immediately, they blame Moses and accuse him of bringing them into the wilderness to die. How apropos is that? How often do we blame others for our troubles, or how often do others blame us for their troubles? I have always said that when we point our finger at someone else, we have three fingers pointing back at us. That truth must be understood by God's people. Even if someone did instigate or say something, we have the free will to choose to listen or not to listen. We always have the choice of our response in all situations. We choose how we respond.

I am sure that most of us can remember the storms after our salvation. The enemy of our soul was not too happy about our changing allegiance. We had finally been delivered from the bondage of a cruel taskmaster, and quickly find ourselves under attack. The questions and doubts almost consumed us. We questioned if we were really saved. Does God really forgive all our sins? Does God really love us? Does the Holy Spirit live in us? The questions and uncertainties were overwhelming storms that plagued us without ceasing. It was the same old same old that Satan trapped Eve with, *"Hath God said?"*

> Therefore whosoever heareth these sayings of mine, and doeth them, I will liken him unto a wise man, which built his house upon a rock: And the rain descended, and the floods came, and the winds blew, and beat upon that house; and it fell not: for it was founded upon a rock. And everyone that heareth these sayings of mine, and doeth them not, shall be likened unto a foolish man, which built his house upon the sand: And the rain descended, and the floods came, and the winds blew, and beat upon that house; and it fell: and great was the fall of it (Matthew 7:24–27).

In this parable, we find the story of the two houses; one was built upon a rock, and the other was built upon the sand. These verses build our understanding of surviving storms. Faith yields the house founded upon the rock when the storm hits. Doubt or unbelief yields the house founded upon the sand when the storm hits. Whenever we question, doubt, or forget what God said before the storm like the Israelites in the wilderness did, we are overcome with fear. The scriptures in Mark demonstrate that fear had the same hold upon the disciples in the ship.

I will unfold more about Joseph, the Israelites, and the disciples as we go on. Many points will become illuminated. But for now, I must keep building. A house cannot be built without a firm foundation. We will dig deeper and deeper, until we have a rock foundation. If we do not grasp the truths necessary to withstand the storms, we will not have the wherewith to stand.

Okay, we see that the Israelites were at the Red Sea. Already, they have forgotten what God had just done in Egypt. They forgot about the plagues and how God spared them. They forgot about the death of the firstborn and how the death angel passed them over. They forgot that they spoiled the Egyptians to come out with great riches (Exodus chapters 7–12). Their rebellion was notorious.

I'm not going to address it all, but I do want to emphasize one point. It was about two years of travelling when they came to Kadesh-Barnea. They were at the place to enter the Promised Land, where Moses sent in the twelve spies to search out the land. When the spies returned, they all bragged about the good land flowing with milk and honey. But ten of them allowed their self-love, their self-preservation, and their lack of faith to be overcome by fear. They claimed the people were strong, the cities are walled, and very great. Moreover, they claimed that they saw the children of Anak who are giants.

We must bear in mind an important fact. They were at the entrance to the Promised Land and refused to go in. The fear of the ten spread to the people who forgot the God who delivered them from the Egyptian bondage, the miraculous crossing of the Red Sea, the healing of the bitter water, the manna falling from heaven daily, and all that God had done. But to me, the most significant factor is the Lord's presence of a cloud by day and pillar of fire by night was there continuously. How did they forget a God whose presence was with them day and night? That is a question that we all could ask ourselves.

They were not like Joseph who kept his devotion to God through storms for more than twenty years. He did not witness the miraculous events that the Israelites did. His faith was based upon the God that he had been told about. Yet, he did not let any voices of fear and doubt influence him. The Israelites had God's presence with them day and night. However, fear and doubt caused them to listen to the ten doubting spies. They ignored the two faithful followers that were telling them the truth. Again, how many times do Christians let fear and doubt cause them to listen to the wrong voices?

Because the Israelites listened to the wrong voices, they did not possess the word or the promise from the Lord. They perished in the storms, and never enjoyed what God had promised. This was no fault of God's. He was more than able to give them the Promised Land. But they did not love God enough to trust him; instead, they listened to the devil's fiery darts. All they did was murmur and complain continually and question God about everything. They were overcome with fear and doubt, until the besetting sin of unbelief consumed them. Only the sin of unbelief kept them from possessing what God had promised. It was not the weights of complaints, accusations, and questions that helped encourage their unbelief; only their unbelief kept them out of the Promised Land (Hebrews 12:1).

Once we understand that the storm is the test of faith that proves the validity of our faith, we see things in a whole new light. Let me explain, when we go to school, we are taught and then tested. It is a constant cycle of being taught and being tested. The test is to reveal to us what we have learned. Whenever God gives a word or a promise, know for sure, the storm or test of faith always follows as certain as the sun rising and setting every day.

Chapter 2

Storms Reveal the Strength of Faith

> Who through faith subdued Kingdoms, wrought righ-
> teousness, obtained promises, stopped the mouths of
> lions, Quenched the violence of fire, escaped the edge
> of the sword, out of weakness were made strong, waxed
> valiant in fight, turned to flight the armies of the aliens
> (Hebrews 11:33–34).

IN THIS CHAPTER, I will continue to build upon the fact that the
storms or the tests of faith always follow the word or the promise
from God as sure as the sun rises and sets each day. However, I
will go a step further and reveal that it is not only the word or the
promise from God, but the revelation read in the Bible, received
through a book, a sermon, a teaching, or anything that reveals a
biblical truth. What we must understand that any spiritual revelation from God can expect a storm to follow. How can we know if
we truly believe it, unless we are tested?

Mark 4:35–40 brings to light that the storm always tries to
overtake us whenever we endeavor to do God's will. The disciples
were smack dab in the middle of obeying Christ's word to cross
over to the other side. We must comprehend the fact that when we
are doing his will, or we have just received a revelation, the storm
will appear. There is no way around it, no way over it, and no way
to escape it. There is only one way to reach the other side, we must

go through the storm. We must endure it, and we must conquer it. It is essential that we survive the storms.

The storms always bring to light our strength of faith. If we are not willing to persist, we will not endure or outlast the storms. I must reiterate that storms or the tests of faith validate what we have learned. Most of us never enjoyed the exams in school, especially the final exams. And make no mistake about it; we do not delight in storms. However, this book is not concerned with our likes and dislikes about storms. It is meant to teach us how to make it through to the end.

In Mark 4:38, we find Jesus asleep on a pillow while the storm is violently attacking; it is out to destroy. Yet, it has no effect on Jesus. He is asleep, whereas, the disciples are in a frenzy of fear. They are beside themselves. Terror has engulfed them with its fury.

In the first chapter, we saw the response during storms between Joseph in Egypt and the Israelites in the wilderness. It was the difference between strong faith and weak faith. Here we find that Jesus has strong faith and the disciples have weak faith.

> Now faith is the substance of things hoped for, the evidence of things not seen (Hebrews 11:1).

In this scripture is found the difference between strong faith and weak faith. If we are to endure storms, this verse must saturate our thinking. We must understand that the word *"Now"* in the verse makes it known that it is in this very moment that faith is our substance or assurance of what we do not literally see. In the natural, we do not see the thing promised, but through faith, we believe that the invisible will be made manifest. This is saying that we believe God and not the storm. We believe what we do not see, not what we are seeing.

Again, the difference is disclosed in Matthew 7:24–27 with the parable of the two houses. The house built upon the rock that Jesus is the Christ endures the storms that beat violently against it. However, we must understand that it is not only knowing the truth that Jesus is the rock we build upon, but believing that with God all things are possible (Mark 10:27). We have to believe that

God is more than able to get us through no matter how impossible it seems.

If we don't believe his word, promise, or revelation, we will not receive it (Matthew 9:29). The storm unveils our strength of faith. Only during the storms do we, ourselves, know which foundation that we have built our house of faith upon. This book is meant to give the necessary preparation to be the house built upon the rock.

> So then faith cometh by hearing, and hearing by the word of God (Romans 10:17).

We must grasp hold of the fact that faith feeds on the word of God. If we starve our physical body or feed it junk food, it will become malnourished, sick, and eventually die. Well, our spirits need food (the word of God) to become healthy and increase our faith in God. Howbeit, although we feed our body well, but we do not exercise it, it will become weak and impotent. The same is true of our faith in God. If we feed upon the word of God, but do not use our faith, it will become weak and ineffective. It is the nourishing and exercising of our faith that will build strong faith.

That is why Jesus said in Matthew 7:24–27 that only the one who hears (feeds on the word) and does (exercises faith) will be like the house built upon a rock. This is saying that we must feed our faith with the word of God and then apply it.

Our faith gets a workout during the storms. Without storms or tests, we will never know what we believe. We can all have great faith when we are not being tested, but genuine faith is discovered in the storms. In other words, the mountain top experience is agreeable, but the valley experience is not enjoyable. It is in the valley storms that we discover the strength of our faith.

Only as we use or exercise our faith can it become strong and powerful faith. The Joseph types in Egypt are those of us who through executing faith are enabled to endure or outlast the storms. We allow our faith to be strengthened, and we find ourselves standing on the other side of the storm. The Israelite types in the wilderness are those of us who quit during the storm. We do not allow our faith to be strengthened, and we do not make it to the other side of the test of faith.

The strength of our faith determines victory or defeat during the storm. This truth is made quite clear between Joseph in Egypt and the Israelites in the wilderness during their storms. This book is meant to make known that our thought process or what we believe will determine whether we come through like Joseph in Egypt or fail like the Israelites in the wilderness.

Let me build on what has been revealed up to this point by looking at another scripture.

> But be ye doers of the word, and not hearers only, deceiving your own selves (James 1:22).

A vital point that is communicated in this verse is that hearers only deceive themselves. How many of us have questioned or doubted God and then conned ourselves into thinking that we don't have to do this or to do that? We lie to ourselves and say, "I'm saved, I pay my tithes, and I go to church; surely that is sufficient." We have deceived ourselves by not heeding the whole counsel of God. Consequently, when the storms attack, a great fall takes place.

The doers are not deceived. When we hear what God says, we do it. If He says do that, we do it. If He says don't do that, we don't do it. If He says go there, we go there. Whatever He says, we do. We may not understand, but we know that those who doubt and question his will don't receive. That is the difference between hearers only and the doers of the word. Hearers only of the word collapse, as did the Israelites in the wilderness. Doers of the word endure the storms and are victorious, as was Joseph.

We need to learn from the example of Jesus asleep in the hinder part of the ship. The storm was raging, but it did not have a negative effect on him. He could sleep, because He had total confidence in his Father to get him to the other side. Likewise, we must become skilled at trusting God. This comes through believing his word without any doubts or questions. It is being confident that what He says, He is able also to perform (Romans 4:21).

In the first chapter, Joseph's strength of faith took him through or enabled him to outlast and overcome the incredible storms in his life. Joseph's storms could not sway his trust in God. His faith remained steadfast. Remember that it took over twenty years for him to receive the fulfillment of the word or promise received. There is not a set time frame for receiving.

Some of us are in the waiting mode; God has given us promises that are yet to be fulfilled. If we look at it in the natural, it could seem as if it will never happen. While focusing on the fury of the storm, we are not able to function properly in our daily life. That only makes the storm more violent. We must not think about how difficult the wait is or how we just want to be out of this storm. That line of thinking will always keep us self-centered and cause us to forget that God always performs his word or promise in his time (Galatians 4:4). He is not like us, He cannot lie (Numbers 23:19). When we doubt him, we become like the Israelites who allowed the storm to overtake them through unbelief. This is the time that we need to be like Joseph and overtake the storm by faith.

> And he said unto them all, If any man will come after me, let him deny himself, and take up his cross daily; and follow me (Luke 9:23).

Herein is found the secret to victory or defeat during the storms. It is not denying ourselves when we feel like it, but continuously denying our flesh daily. Our flesh is our carnal appetites and passions that are founded upon the lust of the flesh, the lust of the eyes, the pride of life, and are not of God (I John 2:16).

It can be most agonizing on us to say "No" to our flesh. I am not talking about the need of food, clothing, and that which is necessary to life, but that which could obstruct our spiritual growth. We must not mollycoddle our flesh, when we know it could be detrimental to the temple of God (2 Corinthians 6:16). Perhaps we desire that chocolate cake that we know will spike our sugar level. Perhaps we covet our neighbor's husband, wife, cattle, dog, house, car, or anything that doesn't belong to us. Perhaps we desire to set someone straight when we know that the Lord wants us to be quiet. Perhaps we know the person is not saved, but date him or her anyway. Perhaps we have an affinity with anger, and let it loose without restraint. Perhaps it is something debauched like pornography, forbidden sex, infidelity, or the like. Perhaps it is just lusting after this or that.

If we cannot deny our self or fleshly desires, we will never get through any storm. Let me explain that we cannot get through big storms in our flesh, if we haven't first learned to overcome little storms. For instance, a lack of employment and lack of income had us in an incredible financial crisis. We practically lived on peanut butter because of the financial storm that was raging. We had peanut butter and toast for breakfast. Lunch was peanut butter and jelly sandwich. Dinner was peanut butter and banana sandwich. It was a continuous denial of self. But I know that God calms all storms in his time (Mark 4:39). It means standing like Joseph, until the promise of deliverance from financial difficulty is fulfilled. Only God knows how long that may be. Bear in mind that during a financial storm, there is a constant denial of self. Unless, self-denial has been learned, the storm will overcome us.

Right now some who are reading this book are in a vicious financial storm, but God will never forsake his righteous nor cause their children to be beggars (Psalm 37:25). It is a choice that we must make during the storm. Will we believe God, or will we give into the fear of financial ruin and destruction? This is the time that we must not allow our flesh to take control and become our god. We choose who to believe. If we believe the storm of fear, we will fail. If we believe God, we will reap (Galatians 6:9). Stay with me to the end of the book, and I believe the wherewith or key to overcome all storms will be made quite clear.

Faith like Joseph means that we have to learn to endure small tests. He had to first endure telling his brothers about his dreams and his brothers hating him the more. It had to be quite a test of self-denial to not hate his brothers after being sold into slavery, being put into prison, and missing his father. But Joseph mastered each test of his faith, one storm at a time. Joseph's faith was so strong that Hebrews chapter 11 mentions him as one of the Heroes of Faith (Hebrews 11:22).

I will explain what I mean by mastering storms one at a time. In school we don't go from first grade to twelfth grade. We must go through one grade at a time, unless we are a genius. However, it is usually mastering one grade at a time. Once we have mastered first grade, we have to hurdle second grade. This is the way it is with our faith walk; we go from faith to faith (Romans 1:17).

Some of us may have spent more time in one grade than others, but all eventually made it to the next grade. Faith works the same way, some take longer to get to the next level, but all who live by faith will make it to the next step.

Joseph made it from faith to faith by not giving place to unbelief. He did not doubt God and give place to questions that could gender anger. If he had, it would have lead to his berating God for allowing the unjust treatment by others. He did not lean unto his own understanding, and we can be sure that he did not understand any of it. But he did know God, and he trusted him to get him through (Proverbs 3:5–6).

In order to continue this chapter, I must give some more scriptures. It is upon them that I will continue to build our understanding of storms and how to overcome them.

> I can do all things through Christ which strengtheneth me (Philippians 4:13).

When it says that we can do all things through Christ which strengtheneth, it means through Christ who empowers or enables us to do all things. Even though it seems impossible, if we believe him, He will endow us with the ability to endure the storm.

> And he said unto me, My grace is sufficient for thee: for my strength is made perfect in weakness. Most gladly therefore will I rather glory in my infirmities, that the power of Christ may rest upon me (2 Corinthians 12:9).

When it says that his strength is made perfect in our weakness, it is referring to the feebleness of our body, which is our human frailty. The strength of Christ made perfect in us is miraculous power by implying a miracle in itself. It is miraculous power, miraculous ability, and miraculous strength. We cannot conjure up this power, ability, or strength in our flesh. It is miraculous by faith through Christ. Only He can give us such power.

> Now unto him that is able to do exceeding abundantly above all that we ask or think, according to the power that worketh in us (Ephesians 3:20).

Again the power is miraculous, which implies that it is a miracle in itself. This miraculous ability is what enables God to do exceeding abundantly above all that we can ask or think. The fact that it says *"Now"* makes clear that it is right this minute that God is able to do according to the power or miraculous strength at work in us. The result of what God does is according to the power that is working in us at the time. The power is the strength of our faith at that moment.

So far, we have seen the strength of faith at work in Joseph and the Israelites. At this time, we will turn our attention to someone else who had the strength of faith to get through what appeared to be an impossible storm.

> Through faith also Sara herself received strength to conceive seed, and was delivered of a child when she was past age, because she judged him faithful who had promised (Hebrews 11:11).

Faith in this verse is conviction, constancy, and fidelity. Through her conviction, constancy, and fidelity, Sarah received strength to conceive. This is the same strength as in 2 Corinthians 12:9. It is miraculous strength, which implies a miracle in itself. Sarah was well beyond child bearing age. In the natural, there was no way for her to conceive. She needed miraculous strength that would in itself be a miracle. But she believed God who *quickeneth the dead, and calleth those things which be not as though they were* (Romans 4:17). She had a dead womb; she was well beyond child bearing age. But is anything too hard for our God (Jeremiah 32:17, 27; Genesis 18:14)?

How did Sarah receive strength, this miraculous ability, to have a baby at her age? It was through or by her faith, her conviction, her constancy, her fidelity to God. This kind of faith cannot be faked. It is not superficial; it is supernatural. Sarah's faith was convinced that God can do anything. It is not a mere profession, but it is living according to that conviction. It is a steadfast and an unmovable devotion to God no matter how unbelievable something may seem in the natural or visible realm. Without the miraculous strength, that in itself was a miracle, she could not have conceived. Only God can give such miraculous ability.

Let's face it. Joseph could have thought it was impossible for his dreams to ever come to fruition. The word from God could have seemed ridiculous after being sold as a slave, never mind being put into prison. Yet, Joseph remained unyielding in his love for God, his devotion to God, and his trust in God. He did not waiver; he was no reed tossed to and fro. He knew what he believed, and he remained steadfast, unmovable in his fidelity to God. He trusted God and his struggle was not in vain (I Corinthians 15:58).

The strength of our faith is contingent upon what we believe. What is the degree of our conviction, our love, and our trust in God? Do we believe that He is capable of doing what He says or promises?

Let us not forget that it is not only a word or a promise, but a word or promise received through revelation of God's word, a sermon, a book, a teaching, or anything that reveals God's truth. Do we believe its truth or doubt when the storms or tests come? We cannot hide what our heart believes during storms. What we believe in our heart determines whether we stand or fall.

To help us understand the difference between saying that we believe God and actually having complete trust in him, I will give one of my favorite examples.

> A tight rope is placed across Niagara Falls. A man asks the crowd of spectators, "Do you believe that I can walk across and back again on the tightrope?" The crowd all reply in the affirmative. He walks across and back again, and the people are cheering. Next, he asks, "Do you

believe that I can push a wheelbarrow across and back again?" They are excited by this time, and all shout their affirmation. He then proceeds to push it across and back again. The crowd is beside themselves with enthusiasm. They are cheering, clapping, and jumping up and down. Once he quiets the crowd, he asks, "Do you believe that I can push a person in this wheelbarrow across and back again?" The crowd is out of control by this time with shouting and cheering. He then shouts, "Who will be my first volunteer?" A hush falls over the crowd. Complete silence overcomes them. There is no sound, no movement, and no volunteer.

Here we see the difference between little faith and great faith. Storms reveal whether our faith is weak or if our faith is strong. Do we truly trust God? We cannot hide what we believe in our heart during the storms. This is revealed with the crowd at Niagara Falls. They were like the disciples in the ship; they looked at the storm through fear for their lives. We must understand that true faith in God gets in that wheelbarrow. Because we know that we can do all things through Christ which strengtheneth us, we actually allow his miraculous power to be at work in us. The people at Niagara Falls seemed to have great faith, until faith had to be exercised.

Faith is not standing at the Jordan claiming that God will get us across. It is taking the step that God says to take. Our flesh may cringe. But if we have learned self-denial, we will put our flesh, our doubts, our fears, our questions under and believe God. He will show us how to stand until we cross on dry land. Don't get me wrong, I am not saying that God will part it or end the storm immediately. Whatever we need to experience or learn in order to stand on God's word must be done. The length of the storm is not the important factor, but our standing by faith is. Standing by faith is why Joseph made it to the other side of his storms. Standing by faith is why Sarah made it to the other side of her storms.

I want to strengthen these facts through an understanding of another scripture.

And thou shalt love the Lord thy God with all thine heart, and with all thy soul, and with all thy might (Deuteronomy 6:5).

This verse means that we are to love God with our all, our total being. Not anyone or anything is to compete with our love for God. We must understand that the most dangerous competition for our love for God is that of self-love and self-preservation. I will not expound on that truth here, but I will do so in the next chapter.

Okay, the strength of our faith is determined by our devotion to God. The question that we must ask ourselves is who has our fidelity, our loyalty? Is it God, others, or self? That is the crux of the matter. Our fealty, our devotion, our allegiance to God is contingent upon who is number one in our heart. The strength of the faith at work in us right now is determined by our faith in God and in his ability during the storm. It is easy to believe before the test, as was seen in the Niagara Falls crowd. But it is the storms that reveal our true strength of faith, our true devotion, our true love for God, and our true degree of trust in him.

For with God nothing shall be impossible (Luke 1:37).

Faith believes that God can do what seems impossible to us, for with him nothing is impossible. This is faith that believes during the storm. It's faith that knows that without God it cannot be done. We have no power to overcome anything in our own strength. But with God, we can do what seems impossible.

It is not quoting scriptures with no storm raging. Let's be truthful how many times have we quoted scripture after scripture to someone who is the middle of a terrifying storm? We seem to have all the answers. Yet, when we are in a similar dilemma, we respond as if we don't have any knowledge of scripture at all. That is a sad truth, for it is during the storms in our life that we must rely upon the revelations of scripture that we have been given.

Our strength of faith is determined by its use; our faith must have a daily workout. The strength of our faith determines if we outlast the storm like the house built on the rock, or if we cave in and collapse during the storm like the house built on the sand

I want us to understand an important fact. God does not control the strength of our faith. He gave us a free will to choose how much we love and trust him. Romans 12:3 and Luke 17:5–6 make clear that God has given us all a measure of faith and the strength of our faith is not contingent upon the size, but the use. We all have muscles. Nevertheless, some of us are stronger than others because we use or exercise them. The same is true of our faith. We all have faith, but its strength is determined by a good workout.

The strength of our faith is as strong as our love, trust, and devotion to God. Jesus asleep in the boat reveals that his love and trust for God was strong. This gave him strong faith. We saw this with Joseph; he exercised his faith daily through his loving God with all his heart, with all his soul, and with all his might.

Little love for God equals little trust in him, and little trust equals weak faith. This is the strength of the faith of the Israelites or those of us who build our house of faith on the sand. If we do not really love, trust, and believe God, we will not receive the word or promise.

Great love for God equals great trust in him, and great trust equals strong faith. This is the strength of the faith of Joseph or those of us who build our house of faith on the rock. If we really love, trust, and believe God, we will receive the word or promise.

The strength of our faith is always made visible during the storms. This book is meant to produce in us a house that is built on the rock; this is faith like Joseph.

Chapter 3

Storms Disclose Love for God

> For when we were yet without strength, in due time
> Christ died for the ungodly. For scarcely for a righteous
> man will one die: yet peradventure for a good man some
> would even dare to die. But God commendeth his love
> toward us, in that, while we were yet sinners, Christ died
> for us (Romans 5:6–8).

IN THIS CHAPTER, I will continue to strengthen that which has
been previously built. Chapter two touched on the truth that the
strength of our faith is contingent upon the degree of our love for
God. In this chapter, I want to emphasize that all that we do during
storms is based upon our love for God and on our trust in his love
for us.

In Mark 4:38, the disciples exclaim, *"Carest thou not that we
perish?"* This question of doubt declares to us that the disciples had
not yet learned to trust in God's love for them. They were really
expressing their lack of faith. Their question can be interpreted in
this way, "Aren't you concerned about us? How can you love us?
We are about to perish, and you're asleep? Why have you forsaken
us to fight this storm alone?"

It not only illustrates their lack of trust in God's love, but it
also shows that they did not love God enough to trust him. They
had been given the word in verse 35 to *"Let us cross over."* Jesus did
not say, "Let me pass over."

God is love (I John 4:16). This revelation is of the utmost importance. Love is an attribute, a characteristic, a trait, a quality of God. We must understand that as God is holy, merciful, just, etc. He is love. Let me explain what this means.

1. The fact that God is holy means that He is not unholy. He is 100 percent holy.

2. The fact that God is merciful means that He is not unmerciful. He is 100 percent merciful.

3. The fact that God is just means that He is not unjust. He is 100 percent just.

Perceiving these truths will enable us to understand the truth that *God is love*. God is 100 percent love. There is no hate, lack of concern, lack of care, etc. in God. Those are human qualities or traits in our fallen, sinful nature. God's nature is sinless. Thus, God's love is perfect, undefiled, unadulterated, and undiluted love. God's love is not tainted with sin like ours. God's love is not corrupt. God's love is not contaminated. God's love is pure. God's love is unalloyed, which means that God's love is not mixed with anything else. It is 100 percent pure love.

Our love can be mixed with what we feel at the time. We can feel anger, jealousy, bitterness, resentment, hurt, prejudice, and the like. When someone does something to us, we can hold a grudge even after they have asked for forgiveness. We allow our emotions to interfere with our love. Our flesh is incapable of pure love, because our fallen nature has an affinity for sin.

Before I continue, I believe I must interject a vital fact concerning God's forgiveness. It seems that many Christians cannot grasp hold of God's forgiveness, because of a lack of understanding. We must realize what happens when we repent and ask God for forgiveness.

1. He not only forgives us, but cleanses us from all unrighteousness (I John 1:9).

2. He casts our forgiven sins as far as the east is from the west (Psalm 103:12).

3. He blots out our transgressions, and He never remembers them (Isaiah 43:25).

In other words, God wipes the slate clean. He will never use what He has forgiven against us. Only we humans will do that the next time someone does something disagreeable to us. God's love is not mixed with feelings or emotions like ours. His love is 100 percent pure, unalloyed love. We must allow the truth of his love to infuse our thoughts, until we realize that God holds no grudges against his repented child. When we repent, God forgives, and He forgets.

Let's get back to the disciples in the ship. Mark 4:37–38 reveals the reason that the disciples questioned Jesus's love for them when they asked, *"Carest thou not that we perish?"* It is quite clear that they were overcome by fear. At this point, I must take us to another scripture to continue.

> There is no fear in love; but perfect love casteth out fear: because fear hath torment. He that feareth is not made perfect in love (I John 4:18).

All right, we saw that the disciples were overtaken by fright and terror. The ship was full of water, and they feared for their lives. It is apparent that they did not love God or believe and trust in his love for them. Their love was not absolute or undivided at this time in their lives. If it had been undivided, it would have cast out their fear. Instead, they were in torment with fear for their lives.

I will now interject my promise to discuss self-love and self-preservation in this chapter. We must understand that the love of the disciples at this point in their lives was divided between themselves and the Lord. Their self-love and their desire for self-preservation gave way to fear. Fear gave way to doubting God's love. Doubt gave way to a lack of trust or unbelief in God.

The disciples were terrified. They forgot the word that Jesus gave them before the storm, *"Let us pass over."* They forgot that God loved them. They forgot all that He had done previously. They forgot that He rebuked an unclean spirit and ordered it to come out of the man. They forgot that He healed many that were sick of divers' diseases, and cast out many devils. They forgot that He healed the man sick of the palsy. They forgot that He healed the man with the withered hand. We must understand that fear initiates forgetfulness.

We saw fear overtake the Israelites in the wilderness. When that happened, they completely forgot about God's miracles. They forgot about his strong hand of deliverance from the Egyptians, and how He protected them. Because of their self-love and self-preservation, they lacked love for God. Their lack of love caused the storms to generate their lack of faith. Lack of faith or unbelief kept them from receiving the Promised Land.

On the other hand, we saw that Joseph did not forget God. He remembered that God loved him, which enabled him to love and trust God. It was his love of God that gave him the strength of faith to overcome his storms. Joseph was steadfast in his devotion and fidelity to God. He did not stagger in unbelief, and his faith received the promise.

Let me explain that receiving a word, a promise, or a revelation from God is like planting a crop. The time between seedtime and harvest can seem like forever when we are waiting, or we are in the middle of storms. This is where the strength, the force, the endurance, the tenacity, the intensity, the durability of our faith becomes visible. During this time, the strength of our faith will disclose if our love for God is alloyed. In other words, it will reveal if it is mixed or divided between ourselves or God. Self-love and self-preservation cannot be hid during the storm between seedtime and harvest. Whoever is number one in our heart will always be uncovered.

Only if we have truly learned to deny ourselves, as in Luke 9:23–24, will we be enabled to love God as Deuteronomy 6:5 says with all our heart, with all our soul, and with all our might.

We must comprehend that our flesh (self) is our natural habitat or home. We were born with a self-loving, self-preserving, and self-centered nature with its pride of life, lust of the flesh, and lust of the eyes.

That is why it is so imperative that parents teach their children self-denial. It is not natural for them. It must be learned, or they will never be able to overcome the storms of life. Children must learn that just because other children may have something, it is not affordable for this family. Children must learn that just because other children may have something, it may not be acceptable for this family that has chosen to serve the Lord (Joshua 24:24). Children cannot learn what they have not been taught. If we are not taught something, how will we ever learn it?

When it comes to denying self, it means that we must wrestle with what we want verses that which God wants. Our flesh (our old nature) always wants its own way. It does not and will never want what God wants. Our flesh does not want to wait. Our flesh does not want to be inconvenienced. Our flesh always wants the final word. Our flesh constantly wants to be in control. We cannot love God in our flesh. Whatever our old nature desires is contrary to God's will for us.

In John 4:24, Jesus makes it unmistakable that we can only serve, worship, love, and be devoted to God in spirit and in truth. Then in John 6:63, He makes clear that we cannot understand the truths of the word of God unless in the spirit. God's word is life; it is spiritual life. Our human reason and logic can never discern spiritual truth.

We must understand that fleshly or carnal understanding or interpretation of God's word will always encourage false doctrines. A false teaching will always lead us astray. That is how cults get started. It is factual, that some wrong doctrine or incorrect analysis of scripture is what most cults are founded upon.

God cannot be served, worshipped, or loved in spirit and in truth, unless we learn to deny our self what it wants. We cannot have unalloyed, unmixed, undivided love as long as we have self-love and self-preservation. Luke 9:24 makes it obvious that if we try to save our life, we will lose it. But if we give it to the Lord, we will save it. In other words, if we live for ourselves, we lose our life. If we live for God, we will save our life.

Let's go back to the disciples in the ship in Mark 4:38–40. Verse 38 shows us their lack of love for God and their lack of belief in his love for them. Their own life meant more to them than God. Therefore, they did not have the strength of faith to trust God to get them to the other side.

How do I know that they had little love for God? Because in verse 40, Jesus asks, "*Why are ye so fearful? How is it that ye have no faith?*" The degree or strength of our faith during the storm is based upon the extent of our love and trust for God. Is it alloyed (divided) or unalloyed (undivided). Fear is a fleshly response; it is not a spiritual response. Perfect love casts out fear. Their love was divided between self and the Lord. It was not absolute love for Christ and him alone.

The folks at Niagara Falls seemed to have great or strong faith until the storm of getting into the wheelbarrow. All of us can appear to be like that crowd. We can say we love, believe, and trust God. We can quote scripture after scripture and appear to have great faith. But what we do in the storm between seedtime (when the word or promise or revelation is planted) and harvest (when the word or promise or revelation is reaped), discloses our true fidelity and strength of faith.

How many of us have waivered or given up on God after a few weeks, months, or years? Would we wait for twenty plus years or so like Joseph? What makes us give up so easily? This book is meant to address that problem, and show us how to endure all storms.

Let me keep building and explain a little more about seedtime and harvest. If we plant a crop or seed, we do not go out the next day or the next week and expect to harvest. Of course not, that would be ludicrous. We know that we have to water, perhaps fertilize, keep out weeds, and shoo away any varmints. It takes time, sweat, and work to receive a harvest.

The same goes for the seed of a word, a promise, or a revelation planted by God. It is during this time between seedtime and harvest that our faith gets a workout. We have to continue to feed, to water, and to fertilize that seed with the word of God. We have to constantly keep out weeds of doubt, fear, and questions.

However, the most time-consuming effort can be shooing away the varmints who would try to encourage the weeds of doubt and questions. It is usually our family, our friends, our co-workers, etc. that continuously try to get us to doubt God. Seeds of doubt ask if God said it. Will God really do it? Does God really want us to do this or to do that? We have all experienced the Genesis 3:1 crowd, *"Hath God said?"*

I want to keep building by turning our attention to another scripture.

> And let us not be weary in well doing: for in due season
> we shall reap, if we faint not (Galatians 6:9).

This scripture speaks loudly an important truth; it makes known that we can grow weary or lose heart during the storms between seedtime and harvest. From the time that we receive the word from God and its fulfillment, we can give up.

Don't get me wrong, I know that the storms can be horrendous when we find ourselves suddenly ambushed by the enemy; that is the time that our flesh wants to quit. This is especially true when we are in a tossing boat full of water and feeling as if we are going under. But we will never reap or harvest, unless we outlast the storm.

The reason that we lose heart is due to our self-love and self-preservation which yields weak faith. We have weak faith because we have fragile love for God. Our love is divided; it is not wholly devoted to God. We are more concerned about ourselves. Even if it is for others, it is still divided love. Anyway, self-love and self-preservation does not deny self; it gives in to the storm.

Only if we outlast the storm will we reap what God has promised. Pay attention here. The devil does not want us to receive the promise. He wants us more concerned with the storms, the inconvenience, and the hardship on our flesh. We can only endure if we know that God is love. We must know that his love for us is undivided. He died for us by paying the ransom for our sins. He paid the debt that we owe God, and that we can never pay.

The Lord has impressed upon my spirit that many who are reading this do not truly comprehend God's love for them. That is something that I can relate to, for I did not understand his love for some time after I was saved. I knew that my sins were forgiven, but understanding his love eluded me.

I couldn't grasp hold of the truth that God really loved me. It was difficult to believe that He is not a respecter of persons. My humanity didn't know of anyone who was not. Every time I read the gospel of John and saw *the disciple whom Jesus loved,* that convinced me that God loves some more than others. I truly believed that He had favorites.

Once I grasped hold of what John knew, I saw things in a different light. My understanding came to light as I did a study on the Tabernacle in the Wilderness. I will not do the whole study, but I want to bring out briefly the coverings. Every covering reveals the redemptive work of Christ.

I'll show the four coverings from the inside out.

1. The inner covering was beautiful. It was costly. The covering was embroidered with blue, scarlet, and gold and had cherubs on it. It was a splendid piece of tapestry. But the only way to see that inner veil or inner covering was to be inside the tabernacle. That suggests that Christ's beauty cannot be seen until we are completely immersed in him. The inner veil is a type of the fullness, the beauty, the heavenly character of Jesus that cannot be seen or understood until completely in.

2. Over the inner covering was the first covering which was made of goat's hair. It was larger than the inner veil so that it completely covered and hid the inner covering. This suggests that at this covering, the fullness of Christ's heavenly character is not seen. These have grasped hold of the truth that Christ is their escape goat or sin bearer and walk free of the guilt of sin. Yet, they have not entered into the fullness, the full relationship that God desires his children to have in Christ. These comprehend that He took away their sins and that He is their escape goat. They know they are now forgiven

and are no longer guilty of their forgiven sins, but they do not know the beauty of Christ's love for them.

3. The next covering or the second covering was made of ram's skin and dyed red. That speaks of the blood Jesus shed for us; it represents his sacrifice for sin. These know that Jesus shed his blood for them, but they do not recognize his fullness, because they go no further in. These individuals are still living in guilt of their past sins. They have never gone past the fact that when they accepted Christ, their sins were blotted out by his blood. They don't understand the fact that He was their sin bearer and their escape goat. They don't understand that He took away their sins completely. They don't comprehend that what is forgiven is forgotten. The enemy comes along and accuses them about their past sins and they are kept out of the fullness of Christ through constantly living in guilt.

4. This is the outer or third covering made of badger skin. It portrayed Jesus as the suffering and rejected savior of Isaiah 53. He is seen as one who had no beauty that He would be desired. If that is all that they see, they will never recognize that his lack of beauty was so that they could become beautiful to God. This reveals that Christ's beauty is inward not outward; his beauty is only seen as their hearts accept his finished work on Calvary.

The coverings of the Tabernacle reveal that only as we get in under the inner covering can we see the beauty of Christ. In here, we behold his heavenly character and all his fullness. We understand his love for us and what his death really means; it is more than the fact that we are free from sin. The inner covering represents the abundant life that Jesus promised (John 10:10). The life in the Spirit is found in that inner covering as we walk in spirit and in truth. Inside the inner covering, we walk side by side with the Savior fully comprehending who and what He is.

The sad truth is that not many of us get under that inner covering. I was at the second covering of goat's skin. I knew that I was forgiven. I was free from the guilt of my sin, but I was not living in the revelation of his love. That covering stifled my growth and my ability to overcome storms. I needed to get under the inner covering and see the love of Jesus in its fullness. Only the heart experiencing his love will have the strength to overcome storms.

That is what the Apostle John did. He knew his Savior, and he knew his Lord. Until the revelation of the love of Jesus Christ gets us under that inner covering, we will never fully comprehend God's love for us. Only as I did that, did I understand God's love for me. I will keep unfolding until it is made clear to everyone.

A lack of understanding of God's love is why so many of us are living a defeated life. We are at the third, second, or first covering and have not gotten down under the inner covering. Because we are so heavily laden by our storms, we question God's love for us. Sometimes we question if He is really there, because we cannot sense his presence. We give into our doubts and fears, when we should be digging deeper until we get under the inner covering.

When we say that we are the temple of God, we must understand the price it cost Christ to buy us. It is a price that none of us can ever pay. It had to be the blood of a sinless sacrifice. There is not one of us, not even a newborn, who can claim the characteristic of being devoid of sin. Without Christ, we would all be lost and undone without any hope. Jesus loved us too much to leave us in that condition. That is what Calvary is all about. It is the greatest love story ever told.

Without an understanding of how precious we are to Christ, we will never get under the inner veil. We will keep thinking that we are worthless, when Christ wants us to know that we are a priceless temple. He spared no cost in purchasing us. He did not care about our faults, our failures, our flaws, our blemishes, or our sinful condition. He loved us in spite of our condition. He did not die for the godly; He died for the ungodly (Romans 5:6–8).

We are his priceless jewels. All of us who are mindful of him have our names written in his book of remembrance (Malachi 3:16–18). God knows all who are his, and we are dear to him. There are no price tags on God's jewels, because no price can be put on Christ's blood.

We are so precious to God that He brags about his child who obeys and pleases him (Job 1:1, 8; 2:3). These scriptures will be brought out in more detail in chapter five.

In John 13:23; 19:26; 20:2; 21:20, he refers to himself as *the disciple whom Jesus loved*. These verses communicate to us that John understood his worth to the Lord. He comprehended the love of God that was willing to die for him.

How many times have we quoted John 3:16? Yet, do we truly understand its magnitude? We tend to say that God loved the world enough to send Jesus to die for it. But that is a superficial comprehension. We need to understand that Jesus would have died for us as an individual. In other words, He would have gone to Calvary if only one of us would have accepted him as Savior.

Grasping hold of that truth causes us to see just how valuable we are to God. If there was only one of us who would believe, He would have gone to Calvary. He would have suffered such agony for one of us. We are of such value to God; He wants us to live in that revelation. John knew that, and that is why he could call himself the beloved disciple. Each one of us who are covered with the blood of Jesus is *his beloved disciple*.

When I received that revelation, I fell to my knees crying. I was overwhelmed by the presence of his love. I had finally gotten under the inner veil to see him as He truly is. His love is not something that we can relate to, it takes revelation under the inner veil to see his love, his compassion, his mercy, and all that He is.

Once we realize his love and self-sacrifice for us, we will gladly deny our self. We understand his self-denial, and we desire to do whatever pleases him. We no longer place more value on our physical life; we are more concerned about our spiritual or eternal life. When the truth of God's love for us becomes a living reality, it revolutionizes our walk.

Believing in the love of God will overwhelm us. We are humbled that God could love us that much, which causes love to swell up inside of us for him. The degree of believing in his love for us and the degree of our love for him is the difference between overcoming the storms or the storms overcoming us. However, we will not know if it is a living reality until the storms. Only during the storms will we really know if we believe that God loves us.

During the storms between seedtime and harvest is the test of what we believe. Do we really trust God's love for us? Do we really love him with all our heart, with all our soul, and with all our might? If we are a self-lover and self-preserver, it will be uncovered during the storms. This truth was seen in that the Israelites' self-love and lack of love for God was apparent during their storms. The sincerity of Joseph's love for God and lack of self-love was revealed during his storms.

Up to this point, it has been shown that the degree of our faith is contingent upon our belief in God's love for us and our love for him. We saw that Christ was not a self-lover or a self-preserver. All his suffering was for us; such love for us transcends our knowledge. It must come through revelation by the Holy Spirit. Once we receive the revelation of God's love for us, we, as John, will say that we are *the disciple whom Jesus loves.*

Chapter 4

Storms Beget Heroes or Deserters

> And thou shalt love the Lord thy God with all thine heart, and with all thy soul, and with all thy might (Deuteronomy 6:5).

THIS CHAPTER WILL CONTINUE to build upon the previous chapters, while unfolding deeper truths. The degree of our love for God and the degree of belief in his love for us will beget heroes or deserters. Heroes similar to Joseph who are listed in Hebrews chapter 11 or deserters like the Israelites in the wilderness who are not listed in Hebrews chapter 11.

Who do we truly love is the key to overcoming the storms or the storms overcoming us. If we are a self-lover and a self-preserver, our faith will fail us during the storms. If we are a Christ-lover and have learned to deny ourselves daily, our faith will hold out strong during any storm.

It is only as we willingly, of our own free-will, offer ourselves as a living sacrifice unto God will we be transformed in our thinking (Romans 12:1–2). If our life means more to us than our love for God, we will be overcome by self-love and self-preservation when the storms come.

With that said, I will now turn our attention back to the Israelites in the wilderness through the following scriptures, *Psalm 106:7–15; 24–27; 34–37*. These verses help us understand why the Israelites failed in the wilderness.

Verses 7–15 tell us that they did not remember God's word or his promises. They forgot about his great mercies. They forgot about what He did in Egypt. They did not remember that He parted the Red Sea enabling them to cross on dry land. They forgot that the Egyptians trying to pursue them drowned in the waters.

Verses 24–27 show us that they despised the good land; they loathed the Promised Land. They did not believe his word that He would give them the land flowing with milk and honey. Instead, they listened and believed the ten lying spies, and God overthrew them in the wilderness.

In verses 34–37, we see just how backwards they became. These verses can be quite shocking. However, their message should encourage us who are on the path of living Deuteronomy 6:5 and love the Lord our God with all our heart, with all our soul, and with all our might. These verses reveal what happens when we do not live according to Deuteronomy 6:5.

Verse 34 reveals that they did not obey God and destroy the nations. God had specifically warned them of the dangers of the heathen nations and their evil practices. Instead of understanding the jeopardy to their soul, they joined the nations and learned their idolatrous ways. They were snared or entrapped by the wicked habits of those around them.

In learning the idolatrous ways of the nations (the world) that they were to avoid, they sacrificed their children to idols. Let me explain in today's language how Christian parents are sacrificing their children to idols in this day and age.

First, let me turn our attention to another scripture reference before continuing with my above statement. As I said earlier, I must construct with care.

> Wherefore come out from among them, and be ye separate, saith the Lord, and touch not the unclean thing; and I will receive you, And will be a Father unto you, and ye shall be my sons and daughters, saith the Lord Almighty (2 Corinthians 6:17–18).

This scripture teaches that if God is to be our Father, we must separate ourselves from the things that can become a snare. We cannot be a partaker of the evil practices of the world and believe that God is pleased. Let me make clear that a trap like the one in Psalm 106:36 does not happen overnight. It takes time being enticed and lured into the evil that the world is doing all around us, before we are entangled.

When we are born again, we must limit our interaction with anyone who could be one of those who try to discourage us from serving the Lord. We must not partnership with those that could encourage doubt and unbelief. We must also free ourselves of the idols that were part of our life before becoming a Christian. Idols are anyone or anything that take preeminence in our heart. It can be any addiction that has control over us. If we cannot let it go, we are caught in its grip. Therefore, whatever has the power to snare us must be avoided. Not anything or anyone can control us unless we allow it. We have the free-will to reject or accept being ensnared. If we are born again, then He who is in us is greater than he who is in the world.

We must understand that we cannot overcome the storms and temptations of this life if we do not love God more than ourselves. That's why as Christians we must always ask ourselves this question, "Will whatever I allow in my life draw me closer to Jesus or will it draw me closer to the world?" That is the difference between spiritual growth and spiritual demise. If our faith is not growing stronger, it is becoming weaker. Strong faith overcomes storms, and weak faith crumbles under storms.

What I want to do at this time is focus on Psalm 106:37. Here we are told that they sacrificed their sons and daughters to idols. This is where I will explain my statement that Christian parents are surrendering their children to idols.

It is not easy for Christian parents to do what God wants, when his or her child is asking to do or to have what other kids their age do or have. But when Christian parents go against their own conscience, which is based on God's word, they throw their children to the enemy to be destroyed.

No, the children are not being physically destroyed, but they are becoming spiritually bankrupt. On the other hand, they could be destroyed physically if they are doing drugs, alcohol, and sexual sins. Also, if they are watching immoral things or playing games that could corrupt them. These ungodly influences have caused children to steal to get drugs. Furthermore, such corruption is influencing children to kill their peers.

I am not saying that all Christian parents are sacrificing their children to idols; some children are just plain rebellious. Believe me, I've suffered the storms of children choosing to rebel against their parents. My concern here is with those whose parents have been caught up in the things of the world, and their lack of denying themselves is influencing their children to do likewise.

Don't get me wrong, I am not saying that this is done intentionally. It starts off like Lot moving his tent close to Sodom. The world has such an attraction, that it seduces into its conduct. This doesn't happen overnight, any more than Lot moving into Sodom happened suddenly. It takes time to be enticed by the world's forbidden fruit, until the luring causes us to move in.

We can all slip into this mentality, especially when we have been saved for many years. It can be a grind year after year of being ambushed by storms. Understand that worldly enticement is just as much of a storm as any other storm. I believe that anyone of us can become battle fatigued. This can be a dangerous position. At that time, we can turn into self-lovers, and stop denying our flesh what we know is detrimental to our soul. We start to think that this can't be that bad. The degeneration of the world influences us until our beliefs start to deteriorate. We have lowered our standard of living to that of the world with its moral corruption.

Please listen to me; for I know how easy it is. The sad truth is that we don't even know that we are backsliding. For instance, we may think that there is something off color in a certain movie, but we convince ourselves that it does have a good spiritual meaning. In other words, a little arsenic can't be that bad. Howbeit, how much arsenic or poison can we ingest before it kills us?

A little leaven leaveneth the whole lump (Galatians 5:9).

This verse makes clear that if we allow a little worldly (ungodly) influence into our lives, it will consume our whole being. There will be no stopping it from spreading throughout all that we do. We will start to see, to talk, to react, and to think like the lost. The leaven or poison of the world will corrupt our spiritual walk until we are walking in the flesh daily and calling ourselves Christians.

We must understand that when parents lose their first love, they pass their backsliding mentality down to their children. In reality, they are sacrificing them to idols (all that is contrary to godliness). Lot did the same thing by moving too close to Sodom and then moving in. When God was going to destroy Sodom because its sin was very terrible, the angels had to take him by the hand to get him out. His wife had been so tarnished by the world that she disobeyed and looked back. We won't even discuss any details about how depraved his daughters became (Genesis 19:1–38).

Let me turn our attention back to the fact that storms will beget heroes or deserters. In chapter three, I pointed out that it was obvious that the disciples had little love for Jesus and did not trust his love for them. At this time in their life, self-love and self-preservation had control over their actions; they had not yet comprehended the love of God. Thus, when the storm came, they forgot his word to "*Let us*" pass or cross over. This is what happened in Psalm 106; the Israelites forgot that God said that He would give them the Promised Land. They were overcome by fear and rebelled against God. As the Israelites forgot what God had done previously, the disciples forgot what Jesus had done previously.

The Israelites were so self-centered that all they did was murmur and complain about everything. Because of their self-love and self-preservation, they could not take their eyes off the storms. They forgot about God's goodness to them, whereas, they should have been thanking him daily for miraculously delivering them from Egyptian bondage. They should have been praising him daily for parting the Red Sea and allowing them to cross on dry land, while the Egyptians pursuing them all drowned. They should have been thanking him daily for the Manna, but instead they complained that they missed the fish, the cucumbers, the melons, the leeks, and the onions in Egypt (Numbers 11:5–6).

If we fail to remember what God has done, we will begin to follow in the footsteps of the Israelites in the wilderness. We owe him our very life, but weariness causes us to become stingy. We begin to grow weary of serving the Lord and our flesh starts to desire the things of the world that we were delivered from. We begin to think like the world and believe that we owe ourselves this or that. When in the spirit and not the flesh, we know what we deserve. But thanks be to God that He does not give us what we have earned, but that He gives us what we have not earned and what we do not deserve.

What happened to the Israelites would not have happened if they had loved the Lord their God with all their heart, with all their soul, and with all their might, and if they had believed that God loved them 100 percent. When we know that God's love is uncontaminated, it does something in our heart. We become overwhelmed by his love and love for him bursts forth. That love wants to do all it can to please the one who loved us so much that He would die for us.

We must understand that a storm is not only waiting for his word or promise, but living the revelations that we have received before the storm. If the Israelites had given thanks and praise to God daily for all that He had done, they would not have forgotten his word, his promise, or his revelations. What I mean by this is their reaction after crossing the Red Sea. They sang and proclaimed his greatness.

> Who is like unto thee, O Lord, among the gods? Who is
> like thee, glorious in holiness, fearful in praises, doing
> wonders (Exodus 5:11)?

They had the revelation that no other god was like him. Yet, when the storms or trials came, they yielded to their flesh. The enticement of the world overtook them. Forgetting God caused them to actually miss the Egyptian bondage that they had cried day and night to be delivered from. The leaven of the world consumed them, and they were engulfed by the desires of their carnal nature. They missed the Promised Land because they forgot who God was. If God is forgotten, his word or promise will not be fulfilled.

In 1 Corinthians 9:24–27, the Apostle Paul teaches that the world races to win a corruptible crown that will fade away and rot. Yet, even though that is the case, the participants are temperate; they abstain from anything that could hinder their physical body. They restrain from all that could be a hindrance to their winning the competition or the race.

Our race is life threatening; our spiritual well-being is at stake. The race that we are running is not physical, but spiritual. It is essential that we abstain from anything that could hinder us from winning or receiving our crown, our prize, or our reward.

Paul knew this and that is why he kept his body under and brought it into subjection to the will of God. He had to beware of becoming disheartened, dispirited, discouraged, depressed, or weighed down with the continuous storms that he had to withstand. He knew that if he did not keep his flesh under, after preaching its necessity to others, he would be disqualified from winning his prize. Whatever we believe that Paul meant in these verses is irrelevant. What is important is that we understand that being consumed by the things of this world will cause us to be battered down during the storms and cause us to miss his word or promise for us in this life. It is a matter of loving God or loving ourselves more.

That's why we must never stop being temperate in our desires, restrained in our flesh, and constant in our devotion to God. A Christian must always be self-restraining. As a bridle is put into a horse's mouth to control its direction, we must bridle our wants that are opposite to God's will for our life.

We must understand that our main concern should not be our flesh but our spirit. If we allow our flesh to be pampered and become fat, our spirit will be neglected and become lean. This is like taking a little arsenic or a little leaven at a time, until our flesh rules. Whenever our fleshly desires are satisfied, leanness of soul will happen (Psalm 106:15).

I believe that sometimes the longer that we are saved, the more dangerous the worldly influence or leaven can become. We must continuously bridle our desires with God's word. Galatians 6:9 makes clear that we can become weary in our warfare. When this happens, lethargy sets in; we become sluggish, fatigued, slothful, and apathetic. We just get tired of fighting our carnal nature and give into a little leaven, and a little leaven, and a little leaven until our whole being is leavened by the world or that which is contrary to God.

Matthew 7:24–27 tells us that the storm beat vehemently. This storm was fierce, vicious, violent, and savage on these houses. It was out to destroy, bring to ruin or to annihilate. Nonetheless, the house that was standing after the storm was the one that had dug deep enough to reach the rock.

Let me explain this, unless we are willing to dig deep into God's word, we will never have a firm foundation. Yes, our foundation is that Jesus is the Christ, but it must be a deeper foundation of loving the Lord our God with our whole life and knowing without a doubt that God loves us. Our rock foundation must be our love for Jesus and believing in his love for us.

We must know that Jesus loves us unconditionally, and that when we repent (abstain from the sin), He forgives us. This means that, because of Christ's love for us, our debt of sin has been wiped clean; we are no longer guilty. The revelation of Christ's love will enable us to stand during the storms. How can we stand firm during the tests or workout of our faith, if our love for Christ and believing in his love for us is shaky?

Without God's word revealing his love for us, we would never know it. The greater understanding that we have that God loves us, the more we love him (1 John 4:19). Only the love of God will enable us to have strong faith that believes that He will get us through the storms.

In the third chapter, it was shown that we can never know our degree of love for God or the degree of belief in his love for us until the storms. We saw this truth in Mark 4 when the disciples' self-love and self-preservation caused them to give place to fear, and fear gave place to unbelief in God's love and in his ability.

The storms always come between seedtime and harvest. That means that the storms emerge after the sowing of the seed of God's word, promise, or revelation, and persist until the reaping. They are meant to destroy our faith, our trust, our loyalty, and our love for God. If we understand that, we will not be ignorant of their intention. Only then can we stand against the violent tempest that wants us destroyed, and declare that we will not let go of his love. His love will carry us through to the other side of the storm. We must understand that the love of God is our life boat during the storm.

Let me make clear that the storms between planting and reaping can rage on for days, for weeks, for months, or for years. If we do not continuously feed the seed with God's word to grow strong in our belief that God loves us and increase our love for him, we will crumble like the house built on the sand.

The degree of love for God during the storms will beget heroes or deserters. In the second chapter, we saw that Joseph is listed in the heroes of faith in Hebrews 11:22. He had been given the word, or promise, or revelation from God, and as sure as the sun rises and sets each day, the storms came. But because he loved God and believed in God's love for him, he remained faithful to him through it all. He was standing on firm ground when the storms ceased. Joseph had crossed over to the other side. In other words, he had gone from planting to reaping.

Now, let's look again at the Israelites in the wilderness who are not found in the eleventh chapter of Hebrews. They were given the word, the promise, or the revelation that they were to possess the Promised Land. But when the storms came between seedtime and harvest, they died in the wilderness. Unbelief kept them from receiving or reaping. They were self-lovers and self-preservers and allowed fear to rule their decisions. It was fear at every juncture; fear engulfed them at the Red Sea, fear overcame them when they came to the bitter water, fear overtook them when they needed food, and fear kept them from entering the Promised Land after the twelve spies returned.

The golden calf was the epitome of their love of the world; for they wanted gods that could go before them (Exodus 32:1). God had gotten them out of Egypt, but He couldn't get Egypt out of them. That is the way it is with many Christians today. God gets us out of the world, but He cannot get the world out of us. Like the Israelites, the love of self causes us to be overcome by the temptation of the world, and our unfaithfulness to God causes us to become deserters. We leave our first love, and we are devoured by self-love.

We become deserters, because we quit offering ourselves as a living sacrifice to God (Romans 12:1). When that happens we sacrifice ourselves to idols, and then we do likewise with our children. But if we fight our carnal appetites, the world, and the devil, we will overcome the temptations or the enemy's ambushes that are launched our way daily.

Let me make something clear here. The degree of our love for God will be the determining factor that enables us to have the strength of faith to outlast or endure the storms. Our priority is our choice. We decide who we love, serve, and worship. We decide if we read our Bible every day. We decide if we believe its teaching. We decide whether or not to deny self. We decide if we are a hero of faith or a deserter.

The Lord has made it clear that the leaven of the world is taking over the church, and it is strangling spiritual growth out of his children. He watches it happen daily, and He is helpless. He can do nothing about it. He did it all on Calvary. His word is the road map and too many are not following it. It seems that the world's pleasures that will fade away have such an attraction to so many of his children. And no matter how much the Holy Spirit tries to convict of its leaven or its poison, some have chosen to ignore him. They no longer offer themselves as a living sacrifice, but are indulging in the corruption of worldliness all around.

Our choices determine what we believe and what we do. The path we take is our choice. Our free will chooses to love Christ or not to love him. We either head toward Christ, or we head away from him. There is no middle ground in serving the Lord; for that is the place of being lukewarm. God wants us to be cold or hot (Revelation 3:15–16). In other words, according to the theme of this chapter, we are either a deserter (cold) or a hero of faith (hot).

My great expectation for the readers of this book is that all who heed its counsel will have the knowledge, wisdom, and understanding to become heroes of faith!

Chapter 5

Storms Appear Without an Alarm

> But as they sailed he fell asleep: and there came down
> a storm of wind on the lake; and they were filled with
> water, and were in jeopardy (Luke 8:23).

UP TO THIS POINT, we have learned that storms are the test of faith, storms reveal the strength of faith, storms reveal love for God, and storms beget heroes or deserters. It has been revealed that storms can be expected between seedtime and harvest; this is the time from receiving the promise, the word, or revelation until its fulfillment.

The degree of our love for God will be the foundation that either causes us to be a hero or a deserter during the fierce storms like the houses built on the rock or on the sand. The house built on the rock is the house that has been built on living according to Deuteronomy 6:5. Whereas, the house built on the sand is built on self-love and self-preservation.

This chapter will continue to build on the four previous chapters, while unfolding more fully our understanding of the various storms. It is during storms that Christians can find themselves trying to understand justice in the face of such calamity. Therefore, it is imperative to bring out our revelations before the storms; that which we were told prior to the storm.

In Mark 4:37, we find that the disciples in the ship are in obedience to Jesus, when suddenly they are ambushed by a great storm. There was no prior warning or alarm. Of course, today, if there is going to be a tornado or storm in most areas, the alarm goes off to warn us. But God wants us to understand that the spiritual storms in our life will come without a warning. We know that they are coming, but the time will not be known. The enemy of our soul will ambush us when we are not expecting the entrapment; that is why we must be prepared. No ambush or trap of the enemy can be productive unless we allow it. Let me explain about preparation a little. If we are going someplace that will involve walking some distance, and the weather says that it will rain. We may not know what time the rain is coming, but we would make sure that we have an umbrella with us. That is prior preparation.

Although we know that storms follow the promise, the word, or revelation, our prior preparation is the key to outlasting the storm. We saw that the Puerto Ricans were not properly prepared for Hurricane Maria, and the country was quite devastated. It is the same for Christians who do not properly prepare for the storms of this life, the storms will defeat us.

> Whosoever cometh to me, and heareth my sayings, and doeth them, I will shew you to whom he is like; He is like a man which built an house, and digged deep, and laid the foundation on a rock: and when the flood arose, the stream beat vehemently upon that house, and could not shake it: for it was founded upon a rock. But he that heareth, and doeth not, is like a man that without a foundation built an house upon the earth; against which the stream did beat vehemently, and immediately it fell; and the ruin of that house was great (Luke 6:47–49).

The above verses reveal the importance of prior preparation. Whoever builds their house of faith on the rock digs deep into the God's word. We believe that God loves us, and we love God with all our heart, with all our soul, and with all our might. Therefore, when the fierce, violent, and savage storms hit, we are rooted deep in the love of God through a knowledge and understanding of his word. We are doers of the word, and our house of faith is unshakeable during the storms.

Whoever builds their house of faith on the sand does not dig deep into God's word. We don't really believe that God loves us, and we don't truly love God. We don't have roots into the word of God, and, therefore, we lack a knowledge and understanding of his word. We are hearers only of the word, and our house of faith is destroyed during the storms.

This chapter will reveal that there are different kinds of storms that are trying to destroy God's children. I will use scripture to expound the severity, the intensity, and the fury of storms. God wants us to come out of this chapter with a deeper understanding of storms; that's why this chapter will reveal the clout of bodily storms.

At this time, I will point our attention to Job 1:1–2:10. It would be practical if we have a Bible handy to read the scriptures. Job 1:8–12 informs us that Job is perfect, upright, and feareth God. We also see that God is pleased with his servant. But the devil accuses God of putting a hedge of protection around Job and that he only serves him for that reason. In other words, the devil claims that God has made Job's life a walk in the park or a tiptoe through the tulips. The devil further states that if God removed his protective hand that Job would curse God to his face. God gives Satan permission to touch all that Job has, but he cannot touch his body.

Before we go on, let's understand that according to 1:3, Job was the greatest or wealthiest man of the East. There was none superior to Job; this man was prosperous in all things. We had to understand his prosperity in order to comprehend the degree of his loss. Job lost all his flocks, all his servants, and all his children; this all happened in one day (Job 1:14–19). Yet in 1:21–22, we find Job standing after such disaster, and he was worshipping and giving glory to God. This is quite noteworthy in that Job didn't have the Bible and the Holy Spirit didn't live in the Old Testament saints.

Let's continue. We see in 2:3–6 that God is still bragging about his servant Job, and that although the devil moved him against Job without cause, he still held fast his integrity. Satan claims that if Job was touched in his body (skin for skin) that he would give all that he had for his life. The devil says that if his bone and his flesh were touched that Job would curse God to his face. That is the same thing the devil argued in 1:11. Again God puts Job into the devil's hand, but Satan cannot kill him.

Before I go on, I want us to understand that the devil cannot touch, in any way whatsoever, God's child without permission from God. That is the time that the real or true test of our love for God and believing that He loves us is sorely tested. When we feel that all hell has unleashed its fury against us, we know that it is the devil attacking. Howbeit, because we also know that God has given him permission to do so, our faith can be shaken to its core. If we have not dug deep into the word of God to fully comprehend the love of God, we can be demolished like the house on the sand.

Anyway, Job is sorely touched in his body; his bodily suffering is a savage and cruel storm. I must interject here that today bodily suffering is how the devil is afflicting many Christians to cause them to grow weary, to become discouraged, to become depressed, and to lose heart; he wants us to quit the good fight of faith. Yes, the devil has God's permission, but he cannot control our reaction during the storm. Only we can choose to love and trust God. Our reaction is determined by our prior preparation before the storm. How deep have we dug into the word of God? Is our foundation founded upon Jesus Christ and loving him with our whole being and believing that God loves us? Do we comprehend that Christ loves us so much that He gave his life to take the punishment that we deserve for our sins? Do we really understand our worth to God? We were purchased by the priceless blood of Christ. There is no price tag on us; because Christ's blood is beyond price. We are God's priceless jewels.

The awareness of our worth to God helps our roots to dig deep into the love of God. The depth of our roots will determine our outcome through the storms. Prior preparation cannot be overemphasized; for it decides whether we are the house built on the rock or the house built on the sand. Whether we stand or fall during the storms is conditional upon our earlier preparation.

Let's get back to Job. I want us to understand that Job's storms are not the result of sin on his part, any more than Joseph's storms were the result of any sin. Storms are not the result of sin; chastisement is the result of sin. We know if we are in sin and refuse to repent. I will talk more about the difference between storms and chastisement as I keep building.

At this time, Job has lost all his flocks, all his servants, all his children and now is in severe bodily torment. The devil is out to destroy Job's faith in God; he has unleashed the powers of hell against him. The motive of the devil is always to demolish faith in God.

> Yea, and all that will live godly in Christ Jesus shall suffer persecution (2 Timothy 3:12).

This scripture shows the next level of attack on Job. It makes evident that all who live godly in Christ shall suffer, shall undergo, or shall experience persecution, torment, or torture. There is no getting out of persecution if we live a godly life; it can be expected as sure as the sun rising and setting each day.

As if Job hasn't suffered enough, the storms of persecution are added. His first persecution or torment starts with his wife, who should have been his helpmeet. She tells him to just curse God and die (Job 2:9-10). In other words, will you just die and get this thing over with. Job claims that God is in control of every life whether it is for good or for evil times. We must understand that seasons are part of our lives; we all go through summers (no storms) or good times and winters (violent storms) or bad times (Ecclesiastes 3:1-8).

In all that Job has gone through, he did not sin with his lips. But the devil was not giving up, so he instigates Job's three friends, Eliphaz, Bildad, and Zophar, to come and console him; which was actually to persecute him. For seven days, no one says a word. However, in 3:1, Job's agony of soul comes out, and he curses the day in which he was born. Job wishes that he had never been born. In 3:20-21, he laments the fact that he would rather be dead than suffer any longer the storm afflicting his body.

I am not going to do a long dissertation of Job's friends' rebuttal or arguments against him. We all should have read the book of

Job and be aware of their cruel allegation. However, I will point out that his friends all believed that bad things only happen to bad people and good people do not suffer.

The beliefs of Job's friends are revealed by their remarks.

1. Eliphaz claims Job is reaping what he has sown (Job 4:7–8).

2. Bildad claims that God in his judgment took Job's children because of their sins; if Job was pure, God would make his righteousness prosperous (Job 8:1–6).

3. Zophar claims that Job has not received the punishment due to his iniquity (Job 11:2–6)

In short, Job's friends alleged that because his sufferings were so great, he must be a great sinner.

Before I go on, I must interject something at this point. In my introduction, I mentioned that my brother had committed suicide when I was young in the Lord. I did not have the insight into storms that I now have. To make a long story short, I was accused of not fighting the devil for my brother, and that I let the devil steal him. I had no idea he was even thinking of suicide. At any rate, I was beat with blame and condemnation until I was almost destroyed by guilt. This continued until the Holy Spirit in me asked me when I became God. I was taken aback; it shook me out of myself. He then proceeded to tell me that I am not the giver or taker of life; God is. If the devil killed my brother, it was God that allowed it. He explained that my faith was being tested. That revelation helped me to understand that just because a Christian is older in the Lord doesn't make them wiser in the knowledge of scriptures. The reason that I brought this out was to show that we can all have deceived friends like Job. However, it is our responsibility to gain knowledge of scripture, so that deceived friends cannot shake our foundation. It is imperative that we have knowledge of scriptures that will reveal an understanding of God, his love, and his promises.

STORMS APPEAR WITHOUT AN ALARM

At this time, I want to turn our attention to some of Job's remarks to their charges against him, which also brings to light some of Job's revelations of God before the storms.

1. Job claims that it could be the hand of the Lord that has brought his sufferings, because the soul of every living thing is in his hand as well as the breath of all mankind (Job 12:9–10).

2. Even after all he's been going through, Job kept his trust in God. He believed that even if God would slay him, he would trust him. He believed that his cause was just. He knew that God was his salvation. He believed that he could stand before God because he was no hypocrite. In other words, Job believed that he was righteous (Job 13:15–16).

3. Job 19:25–27 are remarkable verses, as they reveal that Job believed that there would be a resurrection from the dead. Although his body would be destroyed by worms, he believed that he would in his flesh see God. Furthermore, he knew that his Redeemer lives and would stand on the earth in the latter day.

4. Job considered God's word greater than his necessary food (Job 23:10–12).

In Matthew 4:4, Jesus is quoting Deuteronomy 8:3. These verses mean that man may feed his natural life by eating bread, but spiritual life is only fed by the word of God. Job knew this truth. All Job's claims are revelations of God. I pointed out earlier about the necessity of remembering revelations of God received before the storms. Let's refresh our memory with some facts revealed in some previous examples.

1. Mark 4:37 made known that the disciples were in the middle of doing God's word, when they are ambushed by a sudden storm that appeared without an alarm. They were overcome with fear because they forgot the revelations of Jesus that they had before the storm.

2. Genesis 37 revealed that Joseph has his dreams and is then
ambushed without an alarm; his storms are severe and
without cause. However, the difference in Joseph is that he
remembered his revelations about God and was enabled to
stand during his storms of faith.

Okay, let's continue with Job. In Job 1:1, 4–5, we see that he
is doing God's will. He is perfect and upright; he shunned evil and
he avoided iniquity. He acts as priest for his family. And to ensure
their spiritual purity, he gives the required offerings to God. He no
sooner does this and the storms started. Job's spiritual storms are
the epitome of what an ambush is; he had no idea that good people
would be overtaken by such adversity. He loses all his flocks, all
his servants, and all his children in one day. We must bear in mind
the fact that Job has not sinned. He is being assailed because he
served and pleased God; he is not being disciplined for sin. Verses
1:8 and 2:3 reveal that God is delighted with Job when the storms
appeared without an alarm. Job is ambushed by Satan with utter
malice because he was pleasing to God.

The book of Job does not make clear how long it was between
Satan's attacks, but we can see in 2:3 that he is still a perfect and
upright man. He was still guiltless of sin when the devil launched
his second assault. But this physical attack is a grievous one. Job is
afflicted with boils from the top of his head to the souls of his feet.
He had to use a potsherd (a piece of broken pottery) to scrape off
the oozing from the boils and to scratch the itching. To show his
grief, he sat down among the ashes that were usually located at the
town dumps.

We have to understand this man's torment. As if he had
not endured enough, his helpful wife tells him to curse God and
die. Then come his friends or miserable counselors to add more
agony to his distress; they take turns accusing and insulting him
round-the-clock.

God finally appears in the whirlwind in chapter 38 to speak to
Job. That is when we realize that although Job had not sinned before his storms, his frequent complaints against God in the second
storm had stepped over the line. He claimed that he was crying out

to God and that He was not listening and was not answering. He claimed that God was trying to find some wrong in him.

Job yearned for death when God had given him life (Job 3:20–22). He reminded his friends of his former life and accuses God of being a Giant who has made him the object of his attack (Job 16:12–14). This was really accusing God of being unjust.

We must see the sin here. Yes, the storms were severe, but love for God must outweigh any raging storm. If we are going to outlast and endure the storms, we must remember that our roots must go so deep into the love of God that we are enabled to stand during the storms. The revelations that God has given us before the storm must be front and center not our flesh and its misery.

I understand this type of storm; I was unable to do anything for about two years after I hurt my neck. I just laid in bed day after day listening to the Bible on tape. Talk about learning how to pray without ceasing. I was baffled, but I couldn't believe that I was to spend the rest of my life in bed. God had called me to minister his word, and I wasn't about to give up.

The pain pills and muscle relaxers prescribed by the doctors made me feel like a zombie; I didn't feel in control of myself. It was then that I asked the Lord for help to get away from the prescriptions; I questioned if there was something nonchemical that I could take that could help my body to be healed. Because He promises to heal, I believed his word of revelation that I had received before the storm.

> And ye shall serve the Lord your God, and he shall bless
> thy bread, and thy water; and I will take sickness away
> from the midst of thee (Exodus 23:25).

Anyway, He gave me the following little song during that time that I sang regularly.

> Jehovah Rapha, that is my name,
> The Lord God that heals thee,
> I'll always be the same,
> So reach out and touch me,

Trust in my word,

I will surely heal thee,

It's a promise I've made.

As I kept singing the song day in and day out, an article on natural supplements came in the mail. I knew it was my answer from the Lord; for I had no idea what they were. In any case, I was given insight as to what to take naturally. It took time for the supplements to work, but I gradually got back to a normal life.

Okay, let's get back to Job. We see that in Job 38 that God appears in a whirlwind. A whirlwind seems apropos; as I am sure that Job felt that he was in a whirlwind. It was through the whirlwind that God proceeded to ask Job a question.

Shall he that contendeth with the Almighty instruct him?
he that reproveth God, let him answer it (Job 40:1-2).

In other words, can anyone who contends with God instruct, teach, enlighten, or show him anything?

Job is humbled and confesses.

Behold, I am vile; what shall I answer thee? I will lay mine hand upon my mouth (Job 40:4).

What Job is saying here is that he will shut his mouth. That is good advice for many of us who like to have the last word, who like to be in control, or who think we have all the answers. There is only one who has the right to the last word, who has the right to be in control, and who has all the answers. We would all be much wiser if we remembered that only Almighty God is omniscient.

In Job 42:1-17, it is made clear that Job truly repents of his not understanding God. Because of his repentance, he is back in right status with God, which is what happens to all who truly repent. Although Job had great revelations, as shown earlier, he was not fully aware of God. He had the misconception that bad things do not happen to good people.

That is the way it is today; some of us think that we are not to go through difficulties. I have heard Christians say that if Paul knew what we know he would not have suffered like he did. What a deception and misunderstanding of scripture. God made clear that Paul would experience pain, and that Paul would be vexed.

> For I will shew him how great things he must suffer for my name's sake (Acts 9:16).

We had better make a serious effort to study our Bible if we are going to rightly divide God's word without shame (2 Timothy 2:15). Job had an excuse for not understanding. He could not read his Bible; for it didn't exist at that time. Because we have access to multiple Bibles, we are without excuse if we do not know what the truth is.

After Job repents, God turns his attention and discourse to Eliphaz and his two friends.

> My wrath is kindled against thee, and against thy two friends: for ye have not spoken of me the thing that is right, as my servant Job hath. Therefore take unto you now seven bullocks and seven rams, and go to my servant Job, and offer up for yourselves a burnt-offering; and my servant Job shall pray for you: for him will I accept: lest I deal with you after your folly, in that ye have not spoken of me the thing which is right, like my servant Job (Job 42:7b-8).

We must understand that Eliphaz and his two friends did not repent of their wrong doing. Only Job confesses and repents of his misunderstanding of God. Therefore, God humbled them. They had to go to Job, who they had been badgering for the whole dissertation, and have him pray for them. They go to Job and he prays for them: after this, God turned the captivity of Job around.

I want to insert something here. This book is to show the many types of storms, but I want to make clear that chastisement is not a storm for pleasing God. Dealing with unforgiveness can be self-destructive. God will reprimand (discipline) his child that refuses to forgive. An unforgiving child is not in storms, but chastisement (Hebrews 12:6). Because God loves us, He must discipline us to wake us up. If He loved us in our sinful condition enough to die for us, who are we to hold grudges and not forgive others

(Matthew 18:23–35)? Scripture makes clear that we are forgiven only as we forgive those who sin against us (Matthew 6:14–15). If we love God, we will keep his commandments or his word (John 14:15; 1 John5:3).

We must see here that Job first had to forgive his friends before things changed. How do I know that Job forgave his friends? It is quite simple. He could not have prayed for them with a heart that God would accept, unless he had forgiven them. That is made clear in Genesis 4:3–5 where God only received Abel's offering after He first had respect unto Abel and then his offering. God always looks at the condition of our heart; man looks at the outward (1 Samuel 16:7).

After Job prays, he was blessed with twice as much as he had before the storm (Job 42:12). Yes, God turned the sufferings of Job around as He turned the sufferings of Joseph around. However, let us not forget what storms they had to endure or outlast before things changed.

It is imperative that we understand that we will go through storms; we will have to endure many kinds of storms. Yet, the ones that touch our physical body seem to be the most difficult at times. But if we don't have storms, we will never know how much we love and trust God, nor will we know whether we have built our house of faith upon a rock or upon the sand.

This is the place to interject another truth. If we are pleasing God, we had better expect storms. When we are doing God's will; the devil will look to discourage us. He wants us to rebel against God like the Israelites in the wilderness.

I want to say again a main point that I want us to remember. We must comprehend that neither Joseph nor Job had the word of God to read about their storms or the storms of anyone else. Yet, they both retained their integrity. We have no excuse for not knowing that God loves us, that He is just, that He is more than able to take us through the fiercest of storms, and that He can cause us to stand through the storms. It is not God that is inflicting us, but the devil who wants us destroyed. He wants us to curse God; he wants our faith in God to weaken.

The devil may do the inflicting, but the choice to curse God is ours. There is no storm that we endure where God has forsaken us; for He will never leave us nor forsake us. He is with us always, even unto the end of the world (Hebrews 23:5b; Matthew 28:20b). These scriptures are telling us that Jesus is with us, as He was in the boat with the disciples. During each and every storm that hits us, no matter how suddenly it comes, Jesus is by our side to give the strength of faith to outlast the storm. He is in the storm with us; we do not go through any storm without his presence. We are the ones who forget that He's there. We cast our eyes on the storm and take them off him.

If we truly believe that God loves us, and we truly love the Lord our God with all our heart, with all our soul, and with all our might, we will not doubt that He is in the storm with us. Faith in him knows that He is there to carry us through when we are too weak to go on. We are not only never alone, but Jesus can feel everything that we suffer (Hebrews 4:15). He knows what storms are all about; all we have to do is read about Gethsemane (meaning winepress) and Calvary in the Gospels to know that truth. He can help us put our flesh under and do the will of God no matter how painful to our flesh. Only as we love and trust Jesus during the storms are we empowered to overcome them.

Storms will come as sure as the sun rises and sets every day, but growing weary, being discouraged, being depressed, and losing heart is our choice. Job did fine in the storms where he lost all his flocks, all his servants, and all his children, but when the storm attacked him physically, his lack of knowledge revealed itself.

Many Christians are in storms that are raging against them physically. We must know this and let it sink deep down into our remembrance; storms are not because of sin. Chastisement or discipline is because of sin. This fact is made clear with Joseph and Job. They were not being corrected by God; He was not punishing them. When storms hit, it is because of our uprightness. God is pleased with us, but the devil wants us destroyed. This is made quite obvious in Job. The devil is trying to sift us as wheat; that is why we must stand upon the word, the promise, and the revelations that we received from God before the storm. Even if we are young in the Lord and do not have much knowledge of God's word. He will still have given us what we needed to know before the storm. He will never allow the enemy to attack if He has not given us what we need before the battle. This is seen that when the children of Israel went out of Egypt, they were fully harnessed (Exodus 13:18). That means that they were able bodied soldiers fully armed for battle. That is true of us, if we put on the full armor of God (Ephesians 6:11).

If we don't remember that God loves us, we can, like Job, accuse him of not loving us. We can start to wish that we were dead, when God has given us life. We can accuse God of being unjust. We can berate God for what we believe is his lack of love for us.

The more we serve and please God, we can expect storms. As I said, storms are to give our faith a good workout. A body builder starts with small weights and works his or her way up to heavier and heavier weights. We start with one storm and then two storms and then three storms and so on. If we have not endured the one storm, how will we be able to endure multiple storms at the same time? I will explain the importance of overcoming storms not only in this life, but what they have to do with our reward ceremony at the judgment seat of Christ. That will be in the next chapter; for now let's keep on track with this chapter.

Only if we have dug deep into God's love will we be able to endure the most ferocious storms against our body. If we realize the truth that God will calm the storm in his time (Mark 4:39), we will wrestle with our flesh and hang onto his love until the storm ends. It is important to remember that all storms have an end. The length of the storm depends upon what it takes for us to stand on what we have learned before the storm. As our faith gets a workout during the storm, it will be strengthened.

I must interject something that I believe may be of help. When I was giving a teaching on the difference between storms and chastisement, I said that all storms come to an end. One of my grandsons (Andrew) asked me this question, "If storms have an end, how long does chastisement last?" I told him that was an easy question. It is quite simple; chastisement ends when we repent. If we understand God's forgiveness, we know that we are immediately cleansed, and God does not remember what He has forgiven.

That is the time the devil claims that we didn't really repent and attacks us with storms. We have just pleased God by confessing and repenting, and the devil is livid. He wants us back in sin. If he gets us to sin, we are back in chastisement. We must understand that the devil does not want us understanding God's love; he doesn't want us to experience the beauty of Christ's love found under the inner veil. Once we experience and truly understand his love, we are empowered to overcome all storms.

I understand that there is a lot to take in. But without a thorough understanding of storms and how to be prepared for them, we are defeated before they hit. That was seen when Hurricane Maria hit Puerto Rico and what happened to the Israelites in the wilderness. If we know how to be prepared, we will be ready no matter how suddenly it hits.

Although storms appear suddenly, they are needed to give our faith a good workout. Once we understand that storms are because of our uprightness of heart and that we are pleasing God; we can make it!

Chapter 6

Storms Expose Faith's Maturity

> For whatsoever is born of God overcometh the world:
> and this is the victory that overcometh the world, even
> our faith (1 John 5:4).

UP TO THIS POINT, I have specified that all we do during storms is contingent upon our love, trust, and understanding of God. It is imperative that we understand that truth; success or failure depends upon that foundation. We must also remember that storms are not because of sin; it is the disciplining from God that is due to sin in our life. Furthermore, we must understand that storms are the devil's rage against Christians who are pleasing God; Satan wants our faith in God shattered. The devil claims that if we are put into a troubled sea, we will curse God to his face. In other words, he claims that we will abandon our faith. We cannot overcome storms if our faith is subdued; for without faith it is impossible to please God (Hebrews 11:6).

Just because we know that storms always follow a promise, a word or a revelation from God does not mean that we will receive an alarm. An ambush comes suddenly out of nowhere most of the time. My brother's suicide came without an alarm. Because of that, I believe that the devil brings horrendous storms to pull the foundation from under our feet. He wants us to be so rattled that we don't know what we believe. But that is the time that we have to forget understanding and hold on tightly to God's love. How else could the martyrs for Christ have held out, if not for the love of God permeating their very being?

All storms are meant to quench our faith, but we saw that the most distressing storms can sometimes be the ones that assail our physical body. That is why we must be prepared; our prior preparation is the only barrier against the onslaught that the devil will unleash against us. As I am writing this book, I am reminded of my thesis for my master's degree. I entitled it: *Satan will wear out the saints through sickness and disease.* The reason that I mentioned it is because I believe that God has been showing me for some time that a Christian can become overly conscious of self during sickness and disease. It is quite difficult not to be self-centered when our own body is at war against us. That is when the love of God will verify the maturity of our faith.

In this chapter, I will continue to build upon the previous chapters, while exposing the foundation that received the promise, the word, or the revelation. Our foundation, our substratum, our bedrock, that which we have built upon divulges our degree of spiritual maturity. Our spiritual maturity reveals our footing. In other words, the basis upon which we have built what we believe. We cannot hide what we believe during the storm; for the maturity of our faith will be exposed. If we overcome the storm, our faith has matured. If the storm overcomes us, our faith is immature. It is what we accept as truth that determines our outcome during the storm. Our belief system decides whether we endure or quit. If our faith is built on the rock, we stand firm in the love of God. If our faith is built on the sand, we doubt the love of God. Whether we outlast the storm or surrender to it is dependent on what we truly believe.

Mark 4:35–40 reveals that the disciples had not yet reached spiritual maturity. We find that they had forgotten that Jesus had said to "*Let us*" (meaning all of us) cross over to the other side. They had not yet been rooted in the love of God, and they were still very carnal or fleshly. We must understand that fear can only take us over, if we love our own life more than we love God. Otherwise, why would we fear being with the Lord, unless we loved this life more. Jesus revealed that their fear was due to a lack of faith.

The previous chapters have been illuminating that our faith is only as strong as our love for God and our belief that He loves us. The whole purpose for this book is to prepare Christians for the spiritual ambush of storms. If our faith does not have a workout, it will not become mature or established. That is why I have taken careful steps to build each chapter to unfold the necessity of knowing and believing the love of God. God's love is our bedrock for success during storms.

Perhaps it may seem that I am overly zealous at times, but only the Lord knows which chapter will finally turn on the light bulb of revelation for each reader. I remember when I gave what I considered a simple message to my congregation at the time. A man in his fifties had been in the church all his life, but he had never accepted Christ. Anyway, I preached that Jesus loved us so much that He left Heaven where He was worshipped day and night just to save us. After the message, the man came to the altar with tears streaming down his eyes. He said that he never knew that Jesus was in Heaven before He came to earth. The man was overwhelmed that Jesus loved him so much that He would leave Heaven to come and live here in all this mess. He was wonderfully born again that day to the glory of God. I told that story because it must be understood that not all are at the same level of understanding. Only God knows what will touch each heart.

With that said, I want to pause and interject an important truth. We must be aware that it takes time to grow as a Christian. None of us mature overnight, any more than a crop that has just been planted grows overnight. We know that it will take a long time of watering, fertilizing, weeding, and keeping out varmints before the harvest is ready. Therefore, beating ourselves or feeling inferior because we believe that others are farther along in their Christian walk is the sin of jealousy; we are envious of what they seem to know, or they seem to be. Factors of their growth can encompass many things. Have they been saved longer? Are they avid readers of their Bible? Have they tried to daily separate themselves from the corruption of the world? Do they pray often? Are they more mindful of the things that please God than themselves? Do they live a life of denying their flesh the enticement of the immorality all around?

Let's turn that around. What are the factors of our growth or the lack of it? How long have we been saved? Are we avid readers of our Bible? Do we make a daily effort to separate ourselves from the corruption of the world? Do we pray often? Are we mindful of the things that please God? Do we live a life of denying the world's forbidden fruit to have access into our life?

Being jealous of someone else and their growth will never help our faith to mature. As a matter of fact, it will stunt our spiritual growth and maturity. Furthermore, it really accuses God of loving them more than He loves us. I pray that chapter three settled our worth to God and that He is not a respecter of persons; God does not choose one of us over another. He deals with us according to our faith; true faith is rewarded (Hebrews 11:6).

If we understand that each one of us will give an account of our life to Christ, we should be concerned about what we are doing (2 Corinthians 5:10). Only what we do matters to God as far as each one of us is concerned. God is not mindful about what others do when it comes to us. We alone must answer for our own good or bad deeds. I will relate a little more about the judgment seat of Christ as we go on in this chapter.

At this time, I will use the parable in Matthew 25:1–13 concerning the five wise and five foolish virgins to explain the importance of faith's maturity in order to be prepared for storms. Please understand that I am taking some license with this parable through the leading of the Lord to impress the importance of prior preparation in this life. It is not only being equipped for storms, but being prepared to receive our rewards and crowns at the reward ceremony that will take place at Christ's judgment seat.

Okay, the parable shows that the Bridegroom came without a warning; we have learned that storms come without a warning. The difference in prior preparation between the five wise virgins and the five foolish virgins speaks volumes. It is apparent that the five foolish did not take being prepared seriously. They were not serious about their commitment to God; these are the foolish that build their house of faith on the sand. Whereas, the five wise knew the importance of being prepared; they were serious about their loyalty to God. These are the wise that build their house of faith on the rock.

I believe the difference in the maturity of faith is that the wise virgins loved God with their whole life. They denied themselves and took up their cross daily; their faith was established. These wanted to please the Bridegroom and constantly made themselves ready. Howbeit, because the five foolish were self-lovers and did not truly love God, their faith was not fully developed. Their love was divided between themselves and God; therefore, they pleased themselves and did only what they thought would get them by.

How many of us are like the five foolish virgins? We try to fool those around us into thinking that we are devoted to God, when we are really faithful to ourselves. However, when the storm hits, we will not be able to hide our foundation. Our lack of love for God will reveal our lack of faith; this will then expose the lack of faith's maturity. Likewise, when we stand before the Lord; our lack of rewards will show who we loved more.

Now, the oil in the parable in Matthew makes clear that without the continuous filling of the Holy Spirit, we will not be prepared. We must be constantly infused with the Holy Spirit in order to be ready for the inconvenient ambush. Only the five wise virgins were conscious of always being filled with the Holy Spirit. They made sure they had additional oil sufficient to refill their lamps in the midnight hour. The midnight hour is the dark time of storms.

The five foolish thought that having their lamp was sufficient enough. They had no extra oil, which meant that once their lamps went out, they had no light when midnight came. They were not ready for the storms. It is important to understand that if we have no additional oil at midnight, we have no light to get us through the darkness. The more of the word of God that we feed on, the more the Holy Spirit can fill us with the knowledge and understanding of God's love. It is the word of God that the Holy Spirit will bring to our memory to light up our path (Psalm 119:105).

Before I continue, I wish to illuminate a truth. Earlier I said that we must all appear before the judgment seat of Christ. Perhaps if we understand this, we will desire to be more obedient to Christ in this life. First, let me explain that this judgment is for Christians (his children). This is where believers in Christ will attend the Heavenly Reward Ceremony and receive crowns and rewards, which will be based upon our good and bad deeds done for Christ. I know it says judgment; but it is not a judging of our sins. This is when the purity of our works done as Christians will be judged.

I want to make something clear at this point. The judgment seat of Christ is not a place where all the Christian's past sins will be displayed for all to see. That is a fallacy and misunderstanding of scripture; it is contrary to the truth of God's word. 1 John 1:9 makes clear that when we confess our sins, we are forgiven and cleansed of all unrighteousness. Isaiah 43:25 confirms that God blots out our forgiven transgressions, for his sake and does not remember them. If He remembered them, we would have to answer for them. But because of Christ's blood sacrifice that we have accepted; our sins are under the blood. *God will not look past the blood of Jesus Christ that has covered our forgiven sins.*

There is no judgment for sins that no longer exist. We must remember that what Christ's blood has covered is covered. When we confess and repent (turn from that sin), the sin is no longer under judgment; we have been deemed innocent. Please do not get this confused with the great white throne judgment that is for the lost who will be judged according to their sins.

Our rewards are based on our prior preparation. Are we like the five wise virgins or the five foolish virgins? It is imperative that we take seriously our rewards in this life; otherwise, we will find ourselves embarrassed at our lack of rewards when we stand before Christ. We must comprehend that those rewards are what we will then lay at our Lord's feet; for without him we could not have received them. I don't believe that any of us who love the Lord would want to stand at his feet empty handed. That is why we have to strive to be wise and not foolish.

We that are born again are covered by the blood of Jesus Christ; He is our Lord and Savior. It is the great white throne judgment where all the sins of the lost will be displayed. The lost are not forgiven, and their sins will be exhibited for all to see. These are not covered by the blood of Jesus; for they have denied him in their lives.

To further help us understand the importance of avoiding sin in this life, I will turn our attention to another scripture.

> So Christ was once offered to bear the sins of many; and unto them who look for him shall he appear the second time without sin unto salvation (Hebrews 9:28).

These words are so marvelous, that it excites my spirit. This scripture teaches that when Christ returns, that we who are looking for him will be without sin. Our salvation will be complete. We will be sinless like him (1 John 3:2). We will never have to wrestle with our flesh to remain in the spirit; we will no longer have a sinful nature. Hallelujah!

The only reason that we go through what we do is owing to the consequences of sin. If there was no sin, there would be no storms. Our faith would not need a workout; it would not have to be strengthened. There would be no self-lovers, self-preservers, or self-pleasers if there was no sin. But if we do not want to be without sin here, how could we think that we want to be sinless there? God created us in his image; we were meant to be holy, righteous, and godly like him. Until we understand that sin is contrary to how we were created, we can never hate and abhor sin in all its facets.

In order to have faith and trust in someone, we must believe that he or she cares about our well-being. If we do not believe that someone loves us, we would have a difficult time putting our life in their hands. That is why God wants us to value his love for us. There is no one else who can love us 100 percent. No matter how much they love us, their love will always have a percentage for themselves, others, or something. God has no self-love, no self-preservation, and no self-centeredness; therefore, his love centers on us. We are number one to God; his love is so infinite that it is beyond our understanding. His self-sacrificing death on Calvary for sinners who deserved death should cause us to love him and desire to do whatever He requests.

We cannot have faith in God to trust him during the storms without faith in his love. But what is faith; do we really comprehend what faith is? I believe that faith is rooted in our heart by the truth that God loves us and not in our mind or reason. Faith is not part of our mental capacity; it must come from our inner most being. Faith in God is a conviction that is not understood by human reason. It is being fully persuaded that He will do what He promised, when all seems impossible (Romans 4:20–21).

The Lord is impressing on my spirit that some are feeling betrayed by him; He wants it made clear that betrayal is not part of his attributes. Judas betrayed him; treachery is a human trait because of sin. God is not capable of sin: He is holy and righteous (1 Peter 1:16). One hundred percent holiness and righteousness cannot have anything else mixed in it. If we prayed for something and did not receive it, it was because it was not his will (1 John 5:14–15). Had it been his will, it would have come to pass. Just because we want something does not mean it is part of his plan for our life. As we draw closer to him, we will discern what is his will and what is not his will. Only He knows what it will take to get us from here to Heaven. Our lack of love for him is what hinders our walk; a lack of love equals a lack of faith. Whatever storm that we were going through at the time was to strengthen our faith; however, our little love for him caused us to have little faith. We wanted things our way and when that did not happen, we failed, or we gave up in the storm. He never fails any of his Children who love him enough to trust him through the fiercest storms. What we think that we need is always based upon our flesh and not our spirit. As parents may know what their child needs, God knows for certain what is needed to get us through to eternal life with him.

Let me interject another true example. When my youngest daughter's only daughter (my seven-year-old granddaughter) past away, my daughter felt the ambush of a terrible storm. She was convinced that God was going to heal Sarah, and when He didn't, she felt her whole foundation tremble. She was so confused that she didn't know what she believed about God. The Lord had me explain that He had healed Sarah, but in his way. We tend to box God into our way of thinking. Just because we don't understand something, and the hurt seems unbearable, God does everything out of his love. He told me to tell my daughter that Sarah was now safe in his arms and was waiting for the grand reunion day when her mother would be with her. I told my daughter that she had to concentrate on overcoming the vicious storm and to fight the enemy and believe in God's love. In overcoming, she would one day be with her beloved daughter. Sarah made it, now she had to.

In chapter five, concerning Luke 6:46–49, it was made obvious that prior preparation is like the house that builds upon the rock or the house that builds upon the sand. Our foundation is what we construct our faith on. Bear in mind that both houses were building upon their foundations. That is the way it was with all ten virgins; they all had lamps. Their lives revealed that when the darkness fell that only the five wise were prepared; they were equipped for the storm. The difference in prior preparation is our life. Are we continuously maturing in our faith by ingesting or feeding on the strong meat of the word or are we continuously remaining babes by ingesting or feeding on milk (Hebrews 5:12–14)?

This is of the utmost importance; it must be understood. If our faith does not mature, we will not discern or recognize what is good and what is evil. When the storm comes, we will begin to blame God or others for what's going on in our lives. Immature faith is the neon sign that we lack love for God.

Only the house of faith that digs deep into the word of God and understands God's love will be enabled to love God with all their heart, with all their soul, and with all their might. As we receive the revelation of the love of God, our roots can go deeper and deeper into the love of God. With the love of God so saturating our very being, our faith matures. Mature faith then gives us the strength needed to outlast or endure any storms.

Howbeit, we must understand that without storms, our faith cannot get a workout. Therefore, when the storms ambush us without a warning, we will come through standing firm in his love. Our faith will be unshakeable; it is the house built upon the rock. It is the wise who have additional oil for their lamps. We were prepared and ready for the storm; our prior preparation of knowing God's love for us and our love and trust for him held firm throughout the storm. We may have been windblown, rustled, or challenged, but we held on to his love until the storm ended.

Without the revelation of the love of God, the maturity of our faith will remain undeveloped. Our roots can only be shallow. Thus, when the storms come without an alarm, we will be uprooted and defeated like the house on the sand. Our house on the sand has a quaking foundation; it is unstable like quicksand. Because we are more concerned with self-love and self-preservation, we will not be prepared.

Faith's maturity or the foundation of the five wise virgins reveals that their roots went deep into the love of God. They sincerely loved God. These are the wise who build their house of faith on the rock. When the Bridegroom appeared unexpectedly, they were ready. The wise had no idea of the time or hour, but prior preparation meant that they had a firm foundation. They were prepared; they took extra oil with them. When the midnight hour or the storm came, they were ready for the dark time.

The lack of faith's maturity or the foundation of the five foolish virgins demonstrates that their roots were only superficial and shallow. They did not love God with all their being. They had self-love and self-preservation obstructing their roots from going deep into God's love. These are the foolish who build their house of faith on the sand. When the bridegroom came unexpectedly, they were not prepared. They had not taken additional oil with their lamps. When the midnight hour or the storm hit; they were overcome by it.

Let's look at a few points from the previous chapters that help us to understand the importance of our foundation or faith's maturity. In other words, what belief system have we built our faith upon? First, we saw that Joseph endured or outlasted severe storms, but his firm foundation of loving God with all his heart, with all his soul, and with all his might enabled his faith to mature in the love of God. How do we know that Joseph loved God more than anything or anyone? His remark to Potiphar's wife made it quite clear where his heart was. How many young or old people today are denying their fleshly appetites to be faithful to God? How many would react like Joseph? The answer lies in our hearts. Who do we truly love? Do we love God or self?

> And we know that all things work together for good to
> them that love God, to them who are the called accord-
> ing to his purpose (Romans 8:28).

Joseph knew that whatever was meant for evil, God meant it for good (Genesis 50:20). This is not saying that whatever we are going through is good in itself. For instance, what Joseph went through was not good in itself. His being thrown into a pit by his brothers, his being sold into slavery by them, his being falsely accused by Potiphar's wife of impropriety, and his being thrown into prison were not good things in themselves. Likewise, my brother committing suicide and my being bedridden, etc. were not good things in themselves. However, the ultimate goal, the crucial purpose of God was to use it for the good of Joseph and myself.

Joseph became the rescue of Israel that could have perished during the years of famine. I believe my trials have been to inspire me to write this book about storms. In its pages are found knowledge and wisdom to help my fellow believers understand their worth to God. Thereby helping them to understand the love of God in order to mature in the faith and overcome the storms that come from the enemy of our soul.

Now, let's look again at Job. His faith seemed to be mature and on a solid foundation when he lost all his flocks, all his servants, and all his children, but when the storm hit or attacked his physical body, he fought to keep his faith in God. But to be fair to Job, we must not forget the important fact that he was under the misconception that bad things do not happen to good people. This belief made his foundation of faith to be built upon a fallacy or misunderstanding, which led him to believe that God was being unjust to him. He knew that he was righteous and served God. It is imperative that we understand that if our foundation of faith is built upon an untruth, it will be unstable and we, like Job, will not outlast the storm without giving a false accusation against God.

Only as we dig deep into the word of God will we know that God is love, that He is righteous, that He is merciful, that He is just, and that He is not a respecter of persons. Without the word, we will not understand that we need the workout of storms to strengthen our faith; the lack of storms will yield immature faith. It is through the exercise of storms that we learn to trust in God's love.

As we study the word, we know that we will have good and bad times (1 Peter 4:12–13). We know that there will be summer and there will be winter. But how we react to the storms that the devil unleashes to destroy our faith is determined by what foundation our faith is built upon. Is it love of self or love of God? Love for self is the sand foundation that will fail during the storms. Love for God is the rock foundation that will endure the storms.

Let me recap that bodily storms can perhaps be the most dangerous of storms. Many Christians can endure all sorts of storms standing on previous revelations from God, as Job did. Yet, when a storm smites us bodily, we fight for a while, but then become discouraged, depressed, and lose heart. We forget God's word, or stop believing it. We no longer believe that all things work together for our good. We no longer trust that we will reap if we don't give up. We no longer believe, or we doubt that God is Jehovah-Rapha, the Lord God that heals. We no longer believe that by whose stripes ye were healed. We begin to doubt the love of God, because we listen to the lies of the devil that wants us to believe that love would never put us through such agony.

If we would take our eyes off self and look to Jesus, we would see storms in a different light. Did God not love Jesus? Is He not the beloved son in whom God is well pleased (Matthew 17:5)? Yet, we find him in Gethsemane sweating drops of blood from the agony in his flesh (Luke 22:44). He had to fight his flesh that did not want to be separated from God. We must understand that it was not that Jesus did not want to go to the cross. The reason that He came here was to save us; He considered his death on the cross a joy (Hebrews 12:2). When Jesus cried out on the cross and asked why God had forsaken him, it was to let us know that when He took our sins upon himself, God had to turn away from him (Matthew 27:46). Jesus had to bear the separation from God, so that we will never have to. If Jesus could suffer all that for us, why do we think that we are to be above affliction?

It is time for all Christians to grow up in the faith and get out of our pathetic pity parties. Without maturing in our faith, we will not overcome the storms that are coming our way. As I have said, if we are pleasing God, we can expect the devil to assail us. Prior preparation is detrimental in enduring the storms. If the devil can get us to doubt God's love for us; we will not love him enough to fight through the assault. If we truly love someone, we are willing to sacrifice our life for them. Jesus laying down his life for us proved who He loves.

Without the firm foundation of belief in God's love and our love for him, we will lose heart and be uprooted by the storms. Job revealed that when our body is being beat and beat, we can become overwhelmed and question God's love, mercy, and justice. However, if our faith has matured in the love of God, we may not understand the storm. But we will understand the love of God which will enable us to stand sure footed during the storm.

God will bring every storm to an end. No storm lasts forever. They all have an end, even nature confirms that truth; Hurricane Maria ended. Whether we outlast the length of the storm is determined by our foundation. If our faith has matured on the solid basis of loving God with our all and standing unshakeable in his love for us, we will be enabled to have the faith that believes his word. We will trust that all we are going through is for our good. We will expect that as we keep fighting, we will reap the promise, the word, or the revelation (Galatians 6:9). We will know that God is our healer (Exodus 15:26). Simply put, because of what we believe, our mature faith will have us standing on firm ground, when the storm has ended!

Chapter 7

Storms Ignite Peace or Fear

> These things I have spoken unto you, that in me ye might
> have peace. In the world ye shall have tribulation: but be
> of good cheer; I have overcome the world (John 16:33).

IN THIS CHAPTER, I will continue to help us understand that the maturity of our faith is based upon our belief in the love of God. Our faith can only be as strong as the strength of our love for God. That is the difference between faith built upon the rock and faith built upon the sand. We cannot be mature in faith if our faith is not established on the rock foundation of the love of God; for all other ground is sinking sand. This profound truth must be established as a reality in our lives; for it determines our overcoming the storms or the storms overcoming us.

That is why our prior preparation cannot be overemphasized. It was shown in Mark 4:35–40 that the disciples' lack of a firm foundation or their building upon self-love and self-preservation ignited fear and not peace when the storm came. Therefore, we must understand what prior preparation means. Do we really understand what it involves? Our understanding determines whether we stay planted during the storms or we are uprooted by the storms.

Let me explain it this way. If I wanted to build a house, what I lay as my foundation would determine the stability of my structure. Now, if I take shortcuts and neglect the importance of my support, my house will not be on solid or firm ground. My house may last for some time; it could even be years. However, sooner or later a storm so violent will impact it with such force that it will be shaken from its base. I will no longer be able to hide the truth of my foundation. It will be made known to all who know me.

We can only hide our foundation for so long before it is uncovered. This is true of the maturity of our faith. Some of us may appear to have great faith. We may even talk great faith, but that doesn't signify that we have a firm foundation. We can all talk the talk; but it is walking the walk that matters. Only storms will expose what our faith is built on, whether it is talk or walk. If our love for God is authentic, we will be standing after the storm. However, if our love for God is bogus; we will be shattered during the storm.

The strength of our love for God is dependent upon our knowledge and understanding of the word of God. My understanding of God's word is what enabled me to get under the inner veil and see his love; I was overwhelmed by it. That's why I want to make clear that we cannot know that He loves us, unless we have a comprehension of the word. If we do not know and we do not believe that He loves us, we will not love him in return. Remember, we love him because He first loved us (1John 4:19).

Upon the verses in Mark 4:35-40, we have been enabled to clarify that storms come like an ambush, the necessity for prior preparation, and the necessity for our faith to have a good workout. Our prior preparation is, in fact, our thinking before the storm. How do we rationalize what we believe? Is our thought process based upon the love of God? Do we believe that He loves us? Do we love him with all our heart, with all our soul, and with all our might? Or is our thought process based upon self-love and self-preservation? Do we put more trust in what we can do than what God can do? Do we love our own life more than we love God? Who has the majority of our thoughts? Is it God or is it our self?

Until we can control our thought process to focus on the love of God and trusting in him to do what He promises, we will continue to build our house upon the sand. We will have no stable foundation. Self is as unsteady as sand. It is completely unstable and cannot be trusted. We change like the wind. God is solid as a rock. He is entirely stable and wholly trustworthy. He is unchange-able (Hebrews 13:8). He will always be the same; He will forever be love, merciful, just, etc.

How many of us love one day and hate the next? How many times have we made promises and have not kept them? I have always held that a man or woman is only as good as his or her word. How many of us have always been faithful to our word? On the other hand, God can only love. He has never reneged on his word or promise. He is as reliable as the sun rising and setting every day. We know it will rise and set. That is the way it is with God; He will never fluctuate.

> For as the rain cometh down, and the snow from heaven, and returneth not thither, but watereth the earth, and maketh it bring forth and bud, that it may give seed to the sower, and bread to the eater: So shall my word be that goeth forth out of my mouth: it shall not return unto me void, but it shall accomplish that which I please, and it shall prosper in the thing whereto I sent it(Isaiah 55:10–11).

God's word sent forth out of his mouth is like the rain and the snow that do not return. They accomplish what they were sent to do, and that is to water the earth so that it brings forth the fruit to give seed to the sower and food to the eater.

Now, what we must understand is that his word, like the rain and the snow, does not return, but accomplishes what He sent it to do. It prospers our spirit to bring forth fruit in our lives, thereby giving us seed to sow in others while also feeding our spirit. Once God's word is sown on good ground, it will accomplish the spiri-tual growth necessary (Matthew 13:8, 23). The efficacy of his word will never be canceled; it cannot be nullified. It will either bring forth mature faith to those who accept it or undeveloped faith in those who ignore it. If we do not read and study our Bible, we will not have the nutrients essential to bring forth fruit from the seed that has been planted. What feeds the seed of God is the word of God. As the rain and snow water the seed planted in the earth to bring forth fruit, God's word feeds and waters the seed of the word of God sown to bring forth fruit.

How can the love of God burst forth in our hearts, if we do not feed the seed of his love? Nothing valuable grows without proper care. During babyhood, childhood, and adolescence, our parents carefully tended to us. They took careful steps to nurture our physical growth so that we would be strong and healthy. As we age, it is then our responsibility to exert the same effort to insure our health. Most of us do try to eat properly, to do some exercise, and get the necessary sleep. Sometimes, that is more difficult for some than for others, but most of us are conscious about our health. That same thoughtfulness should be determined for our spiritual growth. Unless our spirits are properly cared for, we will be spiritually weak and sickly. Proper nutrition is needed for our physical well-being, and proper nutrition is necessary for spiritual well-being. Only the word of God can supply our spirits with the proper nutrients indispensable for proper spiritual growth.

The strength of the love of God working in us is what yields weak or strong faith; our faith is only as strong as our love for God. We cannot have mature faith to get us through the storms, if we do not believe that God loves us. Once we know and believe that God loves us, we know that somehow, He will get us through the storms. We know that He is capable of parting the Jordan for us to walk across on dry land. No storm is too difficult for our God.

Let's turn our attention back to Mark 4:35–40, as these verses reveal what causes fear in a storm. If we know what ignites fear, we can learn to avoid it. In the previous chapters, we learned that everything that we do during any storm is contingent on our love for God and our trusting in his love for us. We saw that the disciples were immature in their faith at that time. They did not understand the love of God. Therefore, when the storm came, they were overcome with fear.

Let me interject something here. If we look at the disciples, they were fisherman by trade. In other words, they knew how to survive on the water. Their natural instinct showed them that they were going to perish. Natural instinct or logic took over instead of faith because of their self-love and self-preservation. At this time in their life, their faith was built upon the sand. Their love of self outweighed their love for God. That is the explanation to what causes fear; it is love of self that ignites fear. Only when we are more concerned about self, do we become fearful. If we truly believe that to be absent from the body is to present with the Lord (2 Corinthians 5:8), what are we afraid of? It must be that we love this life more than eternal life with Christ. That is a hard truth; nonetheless, it is a question that we should seriously ponder.

I am not saying that storms are easy. If they were, I would not be writing this book. What I am saying is that the strength of our faith is governed by its components. Is the main element of our faith the love of God or the love of self? What do we build our faith upon? Is it God's love or self-love? In ourselves, we may not really know that answer until the storm comes. Without the workout of faith that comes through storms, we will not know where our allegiance lies. Are we faithful to God or are we loyal to self?

When we were tested in school what we had learned is what was revealed. Tests do not show what we were taught; for being taught something doesn't necessarily imply that we have learned it. That is the same effect of storms; they expose what we have learned. God may have been teaching us many things, but the test of the storm makes known what we have truly learned. Have we truly ascertained that God loves us? Do we really love God with all our heart, with all our soul, and with all our might? Storms will bring the truth of what we have gained to the surface.

Now, the previous chapters have revealed that storms will ignite peace or fear. Peace outlasts the storms like Joseph, whereas, fear is uprooted and shipwrecked during the storms like the Israelites in the wilderness. If our roots do not go deep into the love of God, we will be easily shaken loose and destroyed. Don't misunderstand me; I am not saying that we won't feel the violence of the storm. Nor am I stating that we will not sense our foundation quake. What I am saying is that we have seen trees almost bowed over under the pressure of a storm, and then they stand upright. They felt the turbulence of the storm, but their roots were so deep that they could not be easily uprooted. They hung on, and so do we who have dug deep into the love of God. Because we know that no tribulation, no distress, no persecution, no famine, no peril, etc. can separate us from the love of God which is in Christ Jesus our Lord, we are more than conquerors through him that loves us (Romans 8:35–39). If we hold onto the love of God, we can conquer anything the devil hurls at us.

Our faith is only as strong as our love for God and belief in his love for us. No other foundation is firm and unmovable. All else is sinking sand. I will state again what I said in the previous chapter. If we do not believe that God loves us, how can we trust him with our life? Will we have confidence in him to bring us through the storm? Only as we have confidence that God's love is his motivating factor for all that He does in our life, will we trust him.

At this time, I will turn our attention to scripture that reveals an incredible storm against three young men and their devotion to God.

> Nebuchadnezzar spake and said unto them, Is it true, O Shadrach, Meshach, and Abednego, do not ye serve my gods, nor worship the golden image which I have set up? Shadrach, Meshach, and Abednego, answered and said to the king, O Nebuchadnezzar, we are not careful to answer thee in this matter. If it be so, our God whom we serve is able to deliver us from the burning fiery furnace, and he will deliver us out of thine hand, O king. But if not, be it known unto thee, O king, that we will not serve thy gods, nor worship the golden image which thou hast set up. And the princes, governors, and captains, and the king's counsellors, being gathered together, saw these men, upon whose bodies the fire had no power, nor was an hair of their head singed, neither were their coats changed, nor the smell of fire had passed on them (Daniel 3:14,16–18,27).

What a testimony of faith in the love of God; these three were not afraid of the storm. It is obvious that they were prepared; their roots went deep into the love of God. Their foundation was sure and certain. There were no variables in their love and trust in God.

These young men had strong faith in God, because they had great love for him and complete trust in his love for them.

It should also be noted that these three were captives in a foreign land; Nebuchadnezzar had ordered the master of his eunuchs to bring certain children of Israel to stand in the king's palace (Daniel 1:3–4). They were now in a strange country that served idols, and yet they had prepared their hearts that they would stay loyal to God. Because of their devotion and steadfastness of faith in him, God gave them knowledge and skill in all learning and wisdom. They were ten times wiser than all the magicians and astrologers in the king's realm (Daniel 1:8–20).

Let's look at what they were about to endure. Don't forget that they were pleasing God and doing his will, when the storm came. The storm of persecution will always follow those who live godly in Christ Jesus. Because of their love and devotion to God, they were about to be cast into a fiery furnace that had been heated seven times more than before (Daniel 3:19). Because their roots were deep in the love God, they were enabled to stand firm in their faith, even in the face of death without fear. God delivered them because of their faith in him (Hebrews 11:6). But as I stated earlier, why are Christians so fearful of their lives? How can any of us who claim to love God be more concerned with this life than eternal life with him? I am not saying that we should be looking for death. But if our life is in danger, why do we revert to fear instead of peace in him? He will either get us through to fight another day or we wake up in his arms.

In chapter three, it was made obvious that there is no fear in love. Complete or established love casts out fear. When we believe in our hearts that God loves us, it changes the way we view storms. We are convinced that God intends for our good whatever the devil means for evil. God wants us on the other side of the storm with stronger faith. Being confident in his love and in his ability is what will enable us to get to the other side of the storm without smelling like smoke. In other words, there will be no harmful residue that we came through the storm.

Understand this, we may feel the intensity of the storm, we may hear its threats; or like the three Hebrew boys, we may see the hot flames, but we will not be abandoned. God is always in the storm with us. He was with the disciples in the ship, He was with Daniel's three friends in the fiery furnace (Daniel 3:23–25), and He is with us in our storms.

We must realize that God never leaves us marooned to fight for ourselves; He is not only a Friend that laid down his life for us, but He will never leave us nor forsake us (John 15:13; Hebrews 13:5). Once the revelation of God's love overwhelms us, our roots will be so deeply entwined in his love that nothing and no one else means more to us. That devotion is what will enable peace to be inflamed in our spirit during the storms, and when that reality is seen by others, our life will draw some to Christ. For who else, but Jesus can give us a peace that passes all understanding during the storms?

Chapter 8

Storms Are Faith's Workout

> That the God of our Lord Jesus Christ, the Father of glory, may give unto you the spirit of wisdom and revelation in the knowledge of him: The eyes of your understanding being enlightened; that ye may know what is the hope of his calling, and what the riches of the glory of his inheritance in the saints (Ephesians 1:17–18).

THIS CHAPTER WILL SUM up as well as continue to build upon the previous chapters. Each chapter has been built to enlighten our understanding of the swift ambush of storms and the importance of prior preparation. We must learn to do all that is within our power to be ready for any storm the enemy may wield our way. Our enemy is ruthless, vindictive, malicious, and vengeful. He hates us, because he hates Christ; he is the enemy of all those who have come in repentance to the cross of Christ.

Because Satan couldn't destroy Christ, he has an all-out vendetta against Christians to cause us to doubt God's love which will demolish our faith. He is trying to sift us as wheat, as he wished to do to Peter (Luke 22:31). This sifting is to tempt us into spiritual bankruptcy. He is out to destroy our faith in Jesus Christ at any cost. After all, if he could entice one third of the holy angels to fall with him to become demons (Revelations 12:4), what makes us think that he will not try to tempt us?

We must realize that most of the time, Satan comes as an angel of light (2 Corinthians 11:14). If we are not grounded in the word of God, he can seduce us with false doctrines, lies, and deceit. That is why it is imperative that we are doers of the word and not hearers only (James 1:22). If we are hearers only, we will deceive ourselves and be easily led astray. We have no solid foundation upon which to stand, we are a house built upon sand. As soon as the storms of the enemy hit, we are shaken and uprooted. Our roots were not deep into the love of God; therefore, we had nothing to hang onto during the storm. And, as the disciples in the ship, we will be overcome by fear.

Once fear gains rule over us, we are out of control. We have allowed our self-love and self-preservation to rule our thoughts. Because we don't understand God's love for us and our value to him, we have not loved him with all our heart, with all our soul, and with all our might. Our house of faith has been built upon a false foundation. If we do not understand God's love for us, we tend to become self-lovers. We become more concerned about us and what we want and not God and what He wants. Because we don't truly believe that God loves us, we do not really care what God wants. Perhaps, we didn't say it outright, but our life has been more self-centered than God-centered. We have been thinking that we are serving God, but we have ignored the influence from the Holy Spirit. Because we have only bothered ourselves with our desires, our needs, and our interests, God had little impact on our decisions. We have made most of our decisions based upon what we think we need or what we want. Now, we are in the middle of storms of finances, family, work, sickness, etc., and we are overcome by incredible fear.

This is when the truth of our foundation comes out. Chapter five revealed that having a wrong interpretation or understanding of God can cause us to become shaken during storms. Job believed that bad things do not happen to good people, and he was incredibly shaken by the storm against his physical body. We have to understand that his incorrect view of God led him to believe that God was unjust. Job did not know that it was Satan buffeting him.

He did not comprehend that the storms are allowed by God to give our faith a good workout. Faith is only strengthened by exercise. Each storm we come through strengthens our belief that God loves us, which in turn strengthens our faith in him and his ability to take us through. We have each previous triumph to keep us trusting him through the next storm.

If our foundation is not the love of God, we, like Job, start to accuse God of not loving us. We charge him with being unjust. However, we need to know that God is using storms to open our eyes to see that our foundation is not based upon his love; whereas, the devil is trying to cause us to completely doubt God's love and just give up. The devil knows that if we quit, we do not receive the word or promise that God had given us before the storm. This was made evident between Joseph in Egypt and the Israelites in the wilderness. Joseph plowed through in faith and received the promise; whereas, the Israelites yielded to unbelief and failed to receive the promise. The key to receiving and not receiving is based upon trusting in God's love through the storm. Joseph trusted in God's love and the Israelites did not believe or trust in God's love. Lack of trust in God's love is why so many Christian's are missing what God has for them; they receive the word or promise and fail during the storm or test of their faith.

Yet, scripture makes evident that there is no person, no thing, no tribulation, no distress, no persecution, no famine, no peril, and no *storm* that can separate us from the love of God that is in Christ Jesus. Unless, we know the truth that nothing can come between us and the love of God; we will not love and trust him with our lives. Our foundation is unstable without knowing that God loves us, and we become distressed during the storms until we lose heart.

The previous chapters make evident that the storms will come as sure as the sun rises and sets each day. There is not a question if the storms will come; the question is whether or not we are prepared. How do we prepare? We must dig deep into the word of God, until we are standing on the love of God. Once our foundation is sure and steadfast in his love, we are prepared for any sudden ambush of storms. I am not saying that we may not be bowed like a tree under its turbulence at first, but we grab onto his love and straighten up.

Because we grasp his love for us, when the storms of finances, family, sickness, etc. hit we have the peace of God that passes all understanding (Philippians 4:7). Because peace rules in our hearts, we rest in his love. There is calm once we know that He loves us, and we know that we love him; He becomes our refuge during the storm (Isaiah 25:4). We hide in his love like in the eye of the storm until it is over, and our hearts are at peace in his love.

Our faith becomes stronger through each storm by loving and trusting God. As we lift weights to strengthen our physical body, storms are the weights lifted to grow strong in our faith. We know that if we stop exercising in the natural, we lose what we had gained. That is why our faith must be continuously given a good workout not to lose the growth that we have gained.

Only by digging deep into the word of God and gaining the knowledge and understanding of the love of God will we have a rock-solid foundation to grow firm and strong upon. This is seen in those of us who stand in the love of God during the storm because we understand the necessity of reading and studying our Bibles. When we are ambushed by storms, we might shudder a little like a tree in a storm, but our roots go too deep into his love to uproot us.

Storms are not merciful. If they were, there would be no chance of wreckage. However, God does not intend them for evil against us, but for our good. Storms are meant to fortify our faith against them. Whether we are the house built upon the sand or the house built upon the rock is our choice. God gave us a free will to choose what we believe and what we do. We can choose to believe his love and be enlightened in knowledge and understanding of him through faithfully reading our Bible and spending time in prayer, or we can choose to be unenlightened about God's love by ignoring reading the word and not praying.

Some may be thinking, we were led to believe that storms only come because we are pleasing God and are in his will. That is true, but some of us have been building upon a fallacy or misunderstanding of God and his love. This is not a sure and certain foundation. Let me make something clear, that any of us who have accepted Christ's sacrifice has pleased God and can expect storms. But, like Job, we may not have a right knowledge of God's love for us or our worth to him, which God wants corrected.

We have been doing God's will without the foundation of his love. We have not been constructing our faith upon a solid foundation of loving God with all our heart, with all our soul, and with all our might. We truly don't understand God's love. This was revealed in Chapter three. I knew that I was forgiven, but I had not grasped hold of God's love. I needed to get under the inner veil and experience God's love like the Apostle John.

We are not aware that we don't understand God's love. I know this to be true; for I was one of us who didn't. However, the devil knows what we build upon. He sees our lack of understanding by the things that we say and do. He sees that because we don't comprehend God's love, we tend to be self-oriented. When he goes to God, he wants permission to pull the rug out from beneath us. His goal is total obliteration of any faith that we may have had. However, God is not allowing the storm for our destruction. His motive is his love. God wants us to realize that without an understanding of his love, we will be crushed during the storms. We will believe that He doesn't love his children. We will believe that we have been abandoned. It's believing in his love with our whole being that will give us the faith to make it through. God's love enabled the three Hebrew boys to come through the fiery furnace, and it is his love that will enable us to get through the most severe storms in our life.

I want to bring out another truth, and that is that the devil does not bring storms against those that are serving him. He has them consumed with self and its pleasures. Yes, I know that some are going through hard times, but it is not storms. Before we were saved, we went through difficult times, but it had nothing to do with pleasing God. All the abuse, murder, drugs, alcoholism, child abuse, divorce, corruption, etc. is the consequences of sin in the world. In chapter six, I said that all that we go through is because of sin; if there was no sin there would be no abuse, murder, drugs, alcoholism, sickness, divorce, disease, etc.

The evil in the world is not storms from God; the world doesn't love, serve, or please God. God does not cause anyone to sin; He gave us a free will to choose to do good or to do evil. Sin is our choice and our choice alone. Because of our free will, we can blame no one but ourselves when we choose to sin. We may have been instigated by someone else, but the choice to do or not to do is always ours.

The difference between our going through hard times before we were saved and going through storms once we are saved is that once we are saved, God is with us in the fiercest storms to help us through. We no longer have to experience fear, because we are never alone. I can't imagine life without him now. To think that some are struggling so much in this life without him to help; it boggles my mind how people can't see their need of him. However, the Lord said that self-worship is why some do not want to worship him. When self-love consumes us, we'll have no other god getting in the way of what we want.

Anyway back to the sin in this world and the suffering by the lost. I think back to the child abuse as a child; my father used a cat of nine tails to discipline. I can remember trying to sit in school, and my back and legs made it almost impossible to sit still and listen to the teacher. My father was quite mentally unstable. If we laughed, we were making fun of him. I will not continue with a negative discourse, but felt that some have undergone the abuse of unstable parents. However, I will mention one other fact confirming my statement of the suffering in the world because of sin. One night, he lined up me, my five siblings, and our mother, against the wall and aimed his gun and was going to kill us. Something like that generates a fear that no child should have to experience. But as long as sin exists, it will not end. However, God in his mercy stopped him; for He knew that I was his future child, as was my mother, my sister and my brothers. Perhaps, that helps some to understand why I didn't understand God's love; I associated him as Father with my earthly father.

Some are probably confused as to how I can claim that God would save all my brothers when one committed suicide. I will explain why I believe that. A couple of months before his death, I had prayed for the Lord to save Raymond. My heart was heavy with a burden for his salvation. The Lord then spoke to my heart and asked me to trust him and believe that Raymond would be his. I felt such peace and assurance. Of course, I had forgotten that promise from God when my brother died. But God is so awesome. After all the guilt and condemnation that the devil had heaped upon me, like Job's friends had done to him, was gone, the Lord again spoke to my heart. He reminded me of his promise before my brother died. Then He asked me to remember the thief on the cross and that Jesus had promised that he would be with him in paradise. I don't understand how, but the Lord showed me that my brother had asked like the thief on the cross before he died. God is not a man that He can lie.

I believe that God wants me to interject something here. There are some who have lost loved ones and are not sure where they are. The Lord wants it known that only He sees the heart before death, and there will be many surprises when we get to Heaven and are reunited with those that we thought didn't make it. God says that it only takes a split second for a heart to be quickened with the truth of who He is. Trust that the seed that was planted burst forth with life before their death. Remember, that with God nothing is impossible!

Anyway, the Lord can take all the brokenness, hurts, and confusion that we had before we knew him and use them for our good once we become born again. I know this to be true. I can look back and see the things that I experienced before him, and He has used them to make me a stronger person in Christ. Plus, what I underwent enables me to help others to understand the love of God, and that the devil hates God's creation. He wants all of humanity to hate God as he does. Therefore, if he can convince us to doubt God's love, he has snared us into his web of lies and deceit.

Before we were saved, some of us may have had some serious wounds to our heart. It was God's love that helped me understand the importance of forgiveness; unforgiveness is a powerful tool the enemy uses to keep us from fully experiencing God's love. If we don't forgive from our hearts, we are not forgiven. No matter how severe the transgression against us, we must remember our transgression and rebellion against God. No matter what we may have done, He forgives and expects us to do likewise. This fact is made clear in Matthew 18:23–35 where a servant (us) owed his Lord (God) a debt that he (us) could never pay. When he asked his Lord to forgive him the debt, he freely forgave him. That same servant went out and found a fellow servant that owed him pittance. He took him by the throat to get his money. When his fellow servant asked for forgiveness, he threw him into prison. Once his Lord heard that he refused to forgive his fellow servant, he had that wicked servant delivered to the tormentors. Jesus finished the parable with this, "*So, likewise shall my heavenly Father do also unto you, if ye from your hearts forgive not everyone his brother their trespasses.*"

Let me explain an important teaching in this parable. When we do not forgive from our hearts, we are tormented by our unforgiveness. We continue to remember the transgression until the hate and anger at the person swells up inside us and consumes us with its agony. Unforgiveness does not affect the individual that we refuse to forgive. It is like a cancer in us that gradually kills all joy; unforgiveness seems to affect everything that we do. It's a large beam that trips us up at every step (Luke 6:42). Unless, we truly forgive from our heart, we will remain in torment for the rest of our life. Forgiveness is for our benefit; we are the winners when we forgive. It is such a release when forgiveness is given from the heart, and the agony of hurt, hate, and anger are finally gone. I think that I have said enough in this book that lets it be known that I understand the torment of unforgiveness.

God is the perfect parent that loves us and does everything to help us overcome in this life. If we have been building upon the sand or a self-love foundation, God can use the storm to steer us in the right direction. He is not allowing the storm to destroy, but to wake us up. God will never break a bruised reed nor quench a smoking flax (Matthew 12:20). Jesus came to restore us to a right relationship with God. All that God does in our life is for that purpose. The storms of adversity can cause us to stop and question what we have been doing. We have allowed ourselves to become out of alignment and need to be realigned.

Please understand that it is through the trials of my faith that I began to understand how the enemy ambushes us with storms. If I did not understand what a storm is, I could not have learned the key to overcoming them. Once I grasped hold of God's love, I had learned how to be victorious. I am not saying that it is not an uphill battle at times, but without storms, my faith could not be strengthened. Because I know this truth, no matter how sudden the ambush may be, I am prepared. If God is for me, who can be against me (Romans 8:31)?

This book's purpose was to enlighten God's children to storms and how to overcome them. It was also necessary to understand that storms are like an ambush; we know it's ahead, but not where or when. The only way for our faith to mature is through faith's workout. But if our foundation is not built on the love of God, we will not overcome the storms, the storms will overcome us.

My prayer for you who have stayed with me until the end of this book is that you have come away with an understanding of your worth and your value to God. I promised to reveal how to overcome any storm that the devil unleashes, and I have kept my word. Only as you realize how precious you are to God can you love him in return. There isn't anything that comes your way in this life that God's love cannot take you through. Trust in his love and not the storm trying to destroy you and you will make it. It is the revelation of his love that has enabled me to overcome severe storms in my life. It is his love that has sustained me, when I felt that I could not go on.

Know this, God's precious child that He loves you and that his love is the rock foundation that enables you to overcome or conquer any storm. For with God nothing shall be impossible to them that trust in his love!